Author of

Willie Mosconi on Pocket Billiards

Winning
Pocket Billiards

Winning
Pocket Billiards

by

Willie Mosconi

Author of Willie Mosconi
on Pocket Billiards

CROWN PUBLISHERS, INC.

New York

*Photography by John Mendicino
of Chicago Photographers*

To the women in my life—Flora, my wife, and my daughters Candace and Gloria—I lovingly dedicate this book.

Contents

Foreword

Tribute to a Champion

IF the Power that allocates talent had decreed otherwise, he might have been W. J. Mosconi, vice-president of the First National. His immaculate good grooming and imperious bearing make him look the part.

Or, had Fate been twisted only slightly, he would likely have been billed "Wee Willie, Song-and-Dance Man"—at least for as long as vaudeville lasted.

Obviously, neither alternative came to pass, and we find "Mosconi, William Joseph—born June 27, 1913, Philadelphia," the opening line in the classic biography of a classic sports champion. If an autograph collector unearths an authentic signature of William J. Mosconi, he will possess a rare find, indeed. The magic name is Willie, and he signs it that way, just as George Herman Ruth made headlines only as Babe.

This, then, is a tribute to Willie, whose book I was privileged to help prepare. It was a labor of personal devotion to a man whose friendship I would have prized under any circumstances. I am thankful Willie never became a bank president or hoofer. I might never have met him in those situations. As it happened, Willie parlayed the fairly common gifts of keen eyesight, delicate touch, and ambition into an extraordinarily uncommon career as King of Pocket Billiards.

Willie has since abdicated the throne, but his lengthy reign will be undisputed as long as big-league sports records are kept. His name is on the books to stay, and if you ask him how he put it there he usually resorts to the convenient and self-effacing phrase of most sports celebrities. "Practice and luck," he will say, and he means it, as far as it goes. But you, as the reader of his book, deserve to know more of the making of this champion.

The story of Willie Mosconi makes a fascinating chapter in the rich folklore of billiards.

The name of Willie's game was pool when he was literally born into it as the first son of Joseph Mosconi, a South Philadelphia poolroom operator with more desire than talent for prize fighting. After one of a series of sound thrashings at the hands of another bantamweight, the elder Mosconi returned to his five-table billiard enterprise determined that neither boxing nor pool would provide life's work for little Willie, then six.

By paternal edict, Willie became a reluctant pupil of two cousins, Charlie and Louie, a headline dance team. To enforce the arrangement and discourage Willie's preference of pool over toe-tapping, Father Joseph locked up the stock of playing equipment when his room was closed. Accepting this challenge, Willie continued to practice pool by pushing rounded potatoes across the table with a broom handle, leaning into his shots from atop an apple box.

The combination of his son's soon discovered industry at pool and his equally fervent dislike for dancing led Joseph to the conclusion that if Willie's precocious talent was pool, then pool it would be, and no more potato nonsense.

At the age of seven, Willie was launched on a round of exhibitions leading to a widely advertised match with another billiard prodigy, ten-year-old Ruth McGinnis. He won easily with a high run of 40. With the praise of an amazed audience still ringing in his ears, Willie "retired."

As he tells it now, "I was disenchanted and confused. Earlier, my dad had tried to prevent me from learning the game, and then he pushed me into it too fast."

At the age of seventeen, the illness of both parents necessitated his leaving high school before graduation. In the depression year of 1929, Willie became an upholsterer's apprentice, starting at $8 a week and dexterously progressing to a piecework job at $40 per week before he was fired. He and his boss exchanged punches in disagreement over Willie's request for a day off to watch the Athletics start winning the World Series.

Jobless and broke, Willie mustered courage, and revived a neglected touch at pool to enter and win a local tournament

An exhibition star at the age of seven, Willie Mosconi is shown with Ralph Greenleaf, then world's champion. Willie's appearance poster carried this accurate prediction by Greenleaf: "Having defeated the seven-year-old Willie Mosconi 50 to 46 I have no hesitancy in saying he will be the future world's champion." *Wide World Photo*

with a $75 first prize. He went on to finish third in the city championship that year. This might be recalled as the year Willie cast the pattern of his life. Yet another circumstance would set the mold.

As the date for 1933 divisional competition approached, leading to the national and world billiards tournaments, Izzie Goodman of Fox Billiard Academy found himself without a promising contestant to sponsor because of the death of Eddie Brown, one of Philadelphia's leading contenders. Since Goodman had no desire to forfeit Brown's entry fee, he chose Willie to carry the Fox Academy colors, and Willie responded by winning his double round-robin series against Andrew St. Jean by impressive scores of 100 to 8 and 100 to 20.

Willie advanced to the sectional tournament in New York City, and, with a borrowed cue, stroked his way to victory over such players as Onofrio Lauri and Charles Seaback. At the

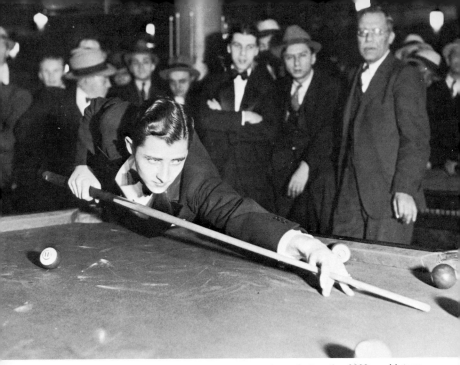

Willie struck a determined pose for photographers during the 1933 world tournament in Chicago. Jimmy Caras, who was to win the title in 1936, watched with arms folded. *United Press International*

national tournament in Minneapolis, won by George Kelly, Willie finished second after a three-way tie for first with George Kelly and Charles Seaback. Second place in the national gave Willie entry into the World Tournament in Chicago.

Against an awesome collection of experienced talent at billiards, Willie finished fourth in the top half of the twelve-man field, which included, among others, Erwin Rudolph (the winner), Ralph Greenleaf, Frank Taberski, Pasquale Natalie, Jimmy Caras, Seaback, Kelly, and Andrew Ponzi. In addition to considerable publicity, Willie was offered an exhibition contract by the Brunswick-Balke-Collender Company, the nation's pioneer manufacturer of billiards equipment.

Under the Brunswick banner, his idol Greenleaf took Willie on a grueling cross-country tour of 107 matches in 112 days. The trek ended with Greenleaf the victor in 57 and Mosconi winning 50, a tally that is a source of pride for Willie equal to any of his later achievements.

"Away from the table, Ralph and I always were close friends, and he even displayed a fatherly interest in my career. But during our matches, particularly those I won, Greenleaf was a fierce and friendless competitor. I learned much from him, including an intense desire to win," Willie remembers.

In world tournaments for the next five years, Willie played well, but failed to crack the monopoly on the title shared by Caras, Greenleaf, and Ponzi. The Mosconi skyrocket appeared to have fizzled in 1939 when he was not invited to compete in the Inter-City league that was to determine the world title that year.

Bob McGirr, one of New York's top billiard promoters, sponsored Willie's return to top competition in 1940, and Willie battled his way through a six-month progression of tournament matches, each one more nerve-jangling than the last. He scored 50 runs of 100 or more balls in his 224 games; finally, the headlines read, "MOSCONI, WORLD CUE KING."

Once he convinced himself the ultimate was possible, Willie made repeating as champion look deceptively easy. After a brief setback, he regained the title in 1942, withstood all challenges from 1943 to 1945, regained the crown from Irving Crane in 1946, and relinquished it only for a year to Caras in 1949. Willie was back on top from 1950 to 1953, and after a one-year lapse in tournament activity he regained the title in 1955 after a few months of supremacy by Crane.

At that point, world-tournament competition in billiards was discontinued for lack of public acceptance and interest. The venerable sport had been saddled with a bad reputation it didn't deserve. By 1960, the game was on the threshold of a rousing comeback, but in the intervening years billiards survived mainly at two extremes. On the one hand, the sport was enjoyed for its fascinating challenge in the exclusive surroundings of private clubs and on college campuses. At the opposite level, it existed as a background for a variety of vices by those who frequented "pool halls."

Throughout those lean years and to this day, Willie Mosconi has maintained a constant faith in the inherent appeal of the game that became his life. He was the goodwill ambassador for billiards when billiards couldn't buy goodwill. Now,

At the age of twenty-eight, Willie won the world's title in 1941. *Wide World Photo*

in testimony to his faith and persistence, the game is making Willie look good as a prophet.

He has always insisted, "In the proper surroundings and with a revival of top competition, billiards will become an even more popular participant sport and spectator attraction than it was when Ralph Greenleaf approached Babe Ruth in both headlines and income."

I'm fortunate. I prize a close personal friendship with Willie Mosconi, billiard champion, missionary, and prophet. I regret only that I was not in his Springfield, Ohio, audience on that night in March, 1954, when he set the yet unbroken

This was a frequent scene in the 1940's and 1950's, with two Willies, Mosconi and Hoppe, sharing the billiard-championship spotlight. Shown here after the 1951 world's competition, Mosconi had achieved his tenth pocket-billiards title and Hoppe had won his eleventh three-cushion crown.

Paul Newman, star of the motion picture *The Hustler*, got expert advice from Willie, who served as technical adviser on the film and executed many of the shots attributed to Newman and co-star Jackie Gleason.

exhibition high run of 526. That unbelievable performance kept him on his feet for three hours. He must have walked three miles, stalking the table with Mosconi intensity, pocketing balls with rapid-fire precision, also a Mosconi trademark.

Will that performance ever be equaled? Perhaps. And if so, I want to be there to experience a thrill second only to knowing, and writing for, the Champion who set the record.

HARRY GROVE

16

Retired now from tournament competition, Willie is busy with a heavy schedule of exhibition appearances.

17

Winning
Pocket Billiards

Tools of the Trade

Introduction to the Table and Equipment

AS in most other sports, equipment for the playing of pocket billiards has undergone refinements through the years. For the most part, however, equipment specifications and game rules have remained standard since the mid-1800's. I feel that an outline of these modern specifications may be helpful to you.

Table specifications: All versions of pocket billiards are played on a rectangular table twice as long as it is wide, with 4½ by 9 feet generally accepted as official tournament size. Finely woven wool cloth is stretched over the rubber cushions and table bed. When this cloth is cleaned, it should be brushed from the head to the foot of the table to keep the nap smooth. The foot end of the table is where the balls are racked.

End rails of the table are marked with three equally spaced diamonds or dots, and side rails are equipped with six such dots to designate playing boundaries and guide the player in computing bank-shot angles. You will learn to use table-rail markers as points of reference as you tackle the fascinating geometry of pocket billiards.

Study the accompanying illustration to familiarize yourself with table markings. Head and foot strings are not drawn on the table, but are only imaginary lines joining specific side-rail dots. Mst pocket-billiards games start with a break shot from behind the head string; this string is also the boundary behind which you must shoot with "cue ball in hand" after a cue-ball scratch or fault. A foot spot is affixed to the table as the center of the imaginary foot string. Balls are racked on this spot to start a game, and during the course of play individual balls that have been pocketed illegally or shot off the

A pocket-billiards table, twice as long as it is wide, is marked by a series of equally spaced rail dots and two string spots. A manufacturer's plate marks the head rail.

table must be returned to the spot or as close behind it as possible if the spot is covered by another ball.

Openings of the two side pockets are about 5½ inches wide, while pocket openings of the four corner pockets are 5 inches wide. Since corner pockets usually afford easier shot angles, their openings are smaller in compensation. The point of difference in side- and corner-pocket openings is to equalize the difficulty in shotmaking.

Racking the Balls: Regulation size is 2¼-inch diameter for all object balls and cue ball. Object balls are numbered 1 through 15, and each ball is of a different solid color or is banded for quick identification. In a later chapter on game rules you will be instructed on how to position balls in the rack by number to start various games. In racking balls, it is important that they be moved to proper position at the foot spot and held in tight formation while the rack is lifted. A "loose" rack, one in which balls are separated, however slightly, will not break properly. Photographs in this section will show you how to rack balls expertly.

In racking the balls, it is important that they be kept in a tight cluster by pressing them forward within the triangle with the thumbs (center), then carefully removing the triangle to keep contact between all balls.

Cues, Mechanical Bridge: Like baseball bats and golf clubs, pocket-billiard cues are available in a variety of weights to suit an individual player's requirements. The average length is 57 inches, and weights vary from 16 to 22 ounces. I use a 57-inch, 19½-ounce cue with a 12½-millimeter tip. As a beginner, you will be well advised to select a medium-weight cue; later, you may experiment with variations when you are able to detect differences in cue action. Many modern billiard centers provide trained instructors to assist players in cue selection. Take advantage of this help.

The length of a billiard cue is a factor in enabling you to reach difficult shots, but situations will arise in a game when neither the cue nor your arms are long enough to make the desired shot. When this happens, use the mechanical bridge without hesitation. I have seen too many players, myself included, occasionally miss a critical shot by stretching into an awkward body position instead of employing the mechanical bridge. Learn to use it; then don't neglect it when it is needed.

Let's move now into succeeding chapters on fundamentals of shotmaking, a section of this book I urge you to read thoroughly and to review frequently as your ability sharpens. There never was a sports champion who dared neglect concentration on the fundamentals of his game. Study, practice, and build on fundamentals for steady improvement in your game of pocket billiards.

Cues are usually stamped by weight in ounces. Most players use a 20- or 21-ounce cue, generally about 57 inches long.

Use the mechanical bridge as a cue support for long shots.

Take Your Cue

Cue Selection, Grip, and Stance

THIS is the first of several preliminary chapters in which I discuss the fundamentals of pocket-billiard play. Forgive the repetition, but I feel compelled to reemphasize the importance of this section to beginner and advanced player alike. I have observed too many otherwise promising students of the game stall and even backslide from a level of ability because of their neglect of fundamentals. A bad habit, formed and not corrected early in a player's development, is likely to hinder his progress forever. Application of proper techniques in the following basic elements will enable you to progress to the maximum of your ability:

1. Cue selection, grip, and stance
2. Basic bridge and variations
3. Stroke and follow-through
4. Hitting the cue ball
5. Basic shotmaking

In this and other sections of the book, I make frequent comparisons between golf, particularly putting, and pocket billiards. I enjoy both sports, and the techniques of play are similar, at least for purposes of illustration. The comparison of billiards to golf breaks down in a hurry on the fairway, but on the putting green the stance, grip, and stroke very nearly duplicate the approach needed on a table with six holes.

The best of putters and billiard players often develop peculiarities in their style. Don't copy these unique characteristics unless you find them most helpful after a long period of trial and error and qualified instruction. Master the accepted fundamentals, and practice. You will be a winner.

Cue Selection: As a beginner, select a cue of average length and weight: let's say 57 inches and 19 or 20 ounces. Later, as you practice, experiment to determine the weight best suited to you. If you find this game as challenging and fascinating as I'm sure you will, your next step may be purchase of a personal cue or rental at your billiard center of one custom-fitted to you.

Find the balance point of a cue by sliding it along your finger until the weight of the butt end equals that of the shaft.

Pocket-billiard cues are nearly six feet long to permit your reaching the maximum number of shots in a comfortable position. Balance is important, too. A good cue is one whose weight distribution permits the player to position his right-hand grip and left-hand bridge properly and without arm strain. This and other references to hand and arm are designed to instruct the right-handed player. You left-handed players, of whom there are a growing number, will reverse such designations.

If you purchase your own cue, use sandpaper to taper the cue tip into a half-moon shape. The cue tip should be rounded, not flat.

Grip Lightly: The "where" and "how" of your right-hand grip at the butt end of the cue are of equal importance. Where you grip the cue determines your ability to stroke freely and smoothly. How you grip the cue is a vital factor in the delicate touch and full follow-through so important to successful shotmaking.

Position the grip; then slide your right hand back three to five inches from the balance point.

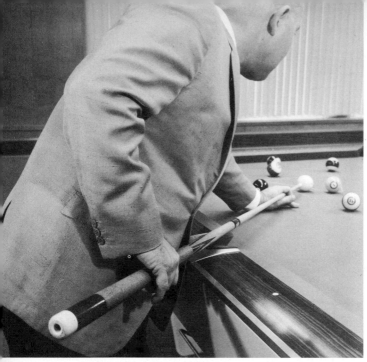

The key to a smooth stroke is a light grip on the cue with the thumb and first three fingers.

First, let us determine where to grip the cue. We start by finding its balance point. Slide the cue across your finger until it balances, with the butt-end weight equaling that of the shaft. Engineers call this the fulcrum point, and youngsters recognize it as the exact middle of a teeter-totter. Now slide your hand three to six inches behind this point to position the grip. Too great a variance from this recommended grip position will either cramp your stroke or extend your stance awkwardly. Both faults are common, but certainly avoidable. Start with the proper grip, then check its position from time to time as you play or practice.

Now for the "how" of a proper grip—and I use that word only because it is in common usage. The word "grip" frequently denotes a firm handshake or tight grasp of an object. Forget both definitions when you approach the grip of a billiard cue. The grip we speak of here is more closely related to that on a teacup handle—delicate, and involving only the thumb and first three fingers.

Illustrations here of the proper cue grip tell the story better than I can with words. I shall elaborate only to spell out the importance of this fundamental. A light and relaxed grip with the thumb and three fingers is the key to smooth and proper cue force in stroking the ball. Stranglehold grips probably are the prime offenders in forcing players into excessive stroke force, one of the most common playing faults. You can produce all the cue force ever needed in this game with a relaxed finger grip and the pendulum action of your right arm.

Let's return to the golf putting green for a comparison. In putting, the left hand guides back the club, and the right hand—gripping the putter with thumb and fingers—moves the club into the stroke. On the billiard table, the left-hand bridge guides the cue, which is moved straight through the stroke with a minimum of right-arm and wrist power.

Mark this down as another frequent checkpoint. As you approach a shot, relax your grip, and then regrip with concentration on thumb and three-finger contact with the cue. Then, to relax further, "waggle" the cue into the stroke as you would in preparation for a golf swing.

Comfortable Stance: I've seen all kinds of stances, and I can safely say there are as many unorthodox stances by billiard players as by subway straphangers. Not all unusual stances are necessarily bad, but many are, and the only way to avoid the risk of an unbalanced stance is to learn the correct position for body and feet—then stick with it.

Here are two points of reference. A good billiard stance puts the player into a balanced and comfortable position, and centers his head over the cue in the line of aim.

How do you achieve a good stance? Eventually, you won't be following this ritual before every shot, but for now, begin by standing erect, facing the direction of your shot. The position of the cue ball will determine how far back from the table you stand. For this exercise in proper form, however, stand about one foot back from the table, with your weight evenly distributed on both feet.

Now, turn both feet slightly to the right and bend forward at the waist. Your feet should be six to eight inches apart

31

To assume a balanced and comfortable stance, begin by facing your shot squarely (top photo), with your weight equally distributed on both feet. Then turn both feet slightly to the right as shown in the lower photo.

With the feet in proper position, bend forward at the waist and bring your head in line over the cue in the completed stance. Your feet should be no more than six inches apart.

and your weight still equally distributed. This accepted billiard stance permits your right arm to swing freely and your left arm to be extended as straight as possible into the left-hand bridge. Your left knee will be bent a bit more than your right, and your body will be free to move slightly forward with the stroke.

The distance of your body from the table must vary according to cue-ball position. A shot with the cue ball at or near the cushion will require assuming a stance farther back. As you stretch for a shot in the middle of the table, of course, your body will be closer to, or against, the table.

Whatever the shot situation, maintain the elements of this basic stance. The keys here are balance, freedom of stroke movement, and position of the head above the cue.

We've come to the bridge; now let's cross it.

This front view illustrates how the proper stance will bring the player's head automatically in line with the cue.

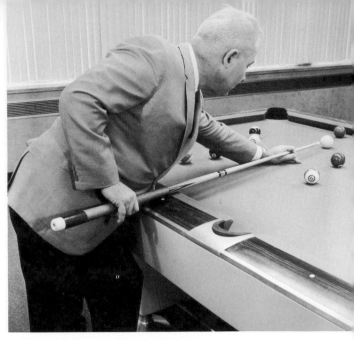

Your body will be close to, or against, the table for shots like this one across the width of the table.

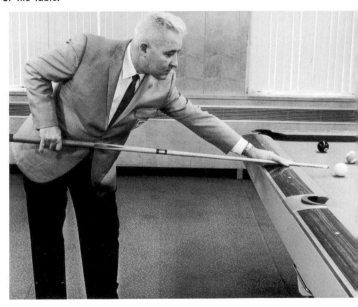

With the cue ball close to the rail, you must take up a stance farther back. The position of the feet and body remains the same.

Construction Ahead

Basic, Rail, and Vee Bridges

A roadway bridge is defined as a firm support structure, and there's no reason to change that definition for a billiard-cue bridge. The purpose of a billiard bridge is to form your hand into as firm and steady a support as possible for the cue, which will travel between your finger structure in stroking the ball. Let's proceed with some basic bridge building.

Basic Bridge: Because the standard bridge is the one you will be using for 90 percent of your shots, it deserves most of your attention and practice. It's as easy as clenching your fist.

In fact, start by making a fist with your left hand. Extend your left arm and place your fist on the table, palm down. Open your thumb and forefinger and lay the cue along your thumb between the knuckles. Draw your forefinger down over the top of the cue and use your thumb to press that fingertip against the middle knuckle of your second finger. You now have a channel through which the cue can slide, but that's not enough. A billiard bridge needs a base of support broader than a fist.

With the heel of your hand resting on the table, separate and extend the last three fingers into as wide an area of support as possible without strain. You now have four distinct and solid contacts with the table and have "built" a sound bridge of finger-girders and a palm-heel pedestal.

If your hand is arched properly, the fleshy part of your thumb will no longer be touching the table, and if your fingers are well spread, the cue shaft will be above the middle of your third finger. Illustrations here from various angles will enable you to compare the bridge you have formed with the one I use. Observe the snug fit of the cue in the channel

To form a basic bridge (top to bottom), make a fist and place it on the table palm down. Open your thumb and forefinger and lay the cue along your thumb. Draw your forefinger down over the top of the cue, then separate and extend the last three fingers into a broad base of support. Note that the hand turns slightly inward at the wrist to complete the bridge.

The cue fits snugly in the channel formed by the thumb and forefinger in these right and left side photographs of the basic bridge. Fingers are widespread but not strained.

formed by my thumb and forefinger. "Snug" in this sense means that the flesh of your thumb and finger moves as you move the cue back and forth in stroking.

Too loose a finger channel is a common bridge fault, as is the tendency of some players to pull their forefinger away from the knuckle of their second finger. Since the bridge is so important a foundation of billiard play, frequently check your hand structure against the photographs in this chapter to make sure you are not straying from proper form.

Before we move into variations, it is well to repeat that the basic bridge is the one that is used most often and that should be used in all possible situations because it is the most dependable. It can be employed with as little as ten inches between the rail and the cue ball.

Once you master the standard bridge structure, you will be ready for later advice on altering it slightly to elevate or lower the cue for special shots.

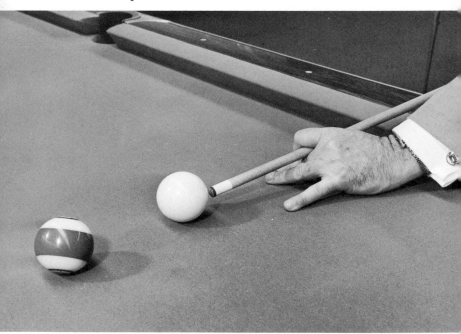

A basic bridge should be used whenever possible, even when the cue ball is as close to the rail as shown here.

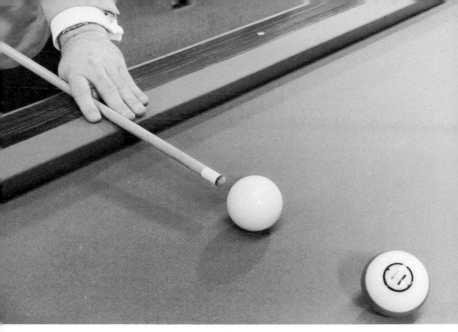

When the cue ball is so close to the rail that it prevents you from using a basic bridge, employ this rail bridge by tucking back your thumb and sliding the cue between your first two fingers.

Rail Bridge: Part of the exciting challenge of billiards is the fact that the player is confronted with shots at all table positions. This often means that the cue ball or object ball may be situated against or too near the table rail to permit use of the basic bridge. We have two solutions to enable us to make these shots.

Assume that the cue ball is two to six inches from the rail— too little table space to form a basic bridge. Tuck your thumb under your forefinger and rest your outstretched fingers and palm on the rail. Separate your forefinger and insert the cue through this channel alongside your thumb. The two fingers and thumb provide points of pressure to guide the cue.

The second rail-bridge situation arises when the cue ball is frozen to the cushion and you face other than a straightaway shot. Use the rail-bridge cue channel between your first two fingers, but rest only your forefinger on the cushion while your other three fingers extend to the table for support.

41

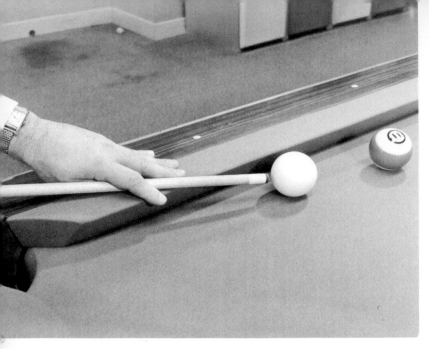

Two other variations of rail bridges show how the forefinger can extend over the rail (top photograph), or how two fingers may rest on the table (lower photograph) for firmer support.

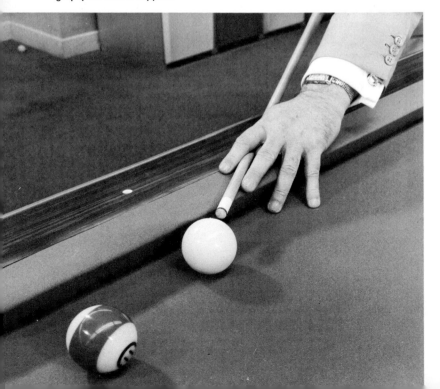

Remember on all rail shots not to elevate the cue more than is necessary.

Vee Bridge: During the course of play, you will be faced with shots in which the cue ball is positioned in front of one or more object balls—too close to hit without elevating the cue markedly. The only solution: elevate the cue.

Without touching any balls (a foul), position your hand behind the intervening ball and arch your wrist by extending all four fingers to the table. In doing so, you no longer have the use of the finger-and-thumb cue channel of a basic bridge. Do the next best thing and form a vee by turning your thumb upward and using it to hold the cue against the top of your hand along the knuckle of the first finger. The cue will slide along this vee and over the obstructing ball as you elevate the butt end of the cue.

Experiment by varying the placement of your support fingers until you determine the arrangement of firmest cue support under these admittedly awkward circumstances.

Mechanical Bridge: We introduce you now to the device mentioned in our chapter on playing equipment. Its simple purpose is to provide cue support for shots too far to reach with your arms. Using it prevents you from committing a foul (not having one foot on the floor as you shoot) and from overextending your arms and body into an unsteady shooting position.

Move the mechanical bridge into position carefully (remember that disturbing balls is also a foul) and hold the handle end firmly against the table with your left hand. Bridge your cue in the appropriate slot, and stroke with a three-finger grip on the butt end. The stroke must be smooth to keep your cue from jumping out of the slot.

Also illustrated here is use of the mechanical bridge to shoot over intervening balls. You would be using the hand vee bridge if this shot were close enough. Since it isn't, turn the mechanical bridge on its side to elevate the cue.

Before we chalk up and stroke, remember that all billiard body positions—stance, grip, and bridge—are designed to keep your head over the cue in line of aim.

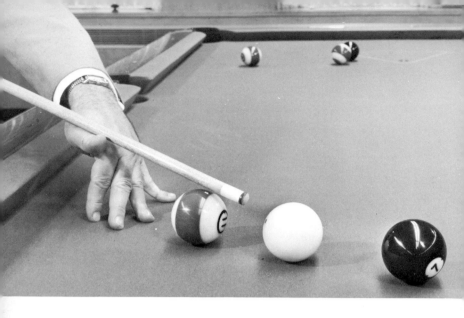

In these shot situations the vee bridge is necessary to elevate the cue over obstructing balls. Use thumb pressure to keep the cue firm in the vee channel.

Use the mechanical bridge to reach long shots. The handle should be held against the table, and the stroke should be made by gripping the cue at the end with your thumb and first two fingers. To elevate the cue (photograph at right), turn the mechanical bridge on end.

A Delicate Touch

Stroke Soft with Follow-through

REMEMBER my comparison of billiards to golf putting? Picture this. An enthusiastic golfer equips himself with the finest of clubs, spends hours at the driving range learning to power the ball 250 yards, dresses in flashy togs, and then never breaks 90 because he three-putts nearly every green. He could better spend his practice time and money learning to stroke rather than jab his putts.

Back to our billiard table, we may find the same enthusiast who has a "picture" stance, grip, and bridge and who has developed a superior sense of aiming, yet seldom is a winner. I'll bet my ivory-inlaid cue his fault lies in his stroke control, speed, and follow-through.

Proper stance, grip, and bridge are vital preparations to effective stroking, but it's your movement of the cue that propels the ball and determines where it rolls dead. We'll devote more space later to a discussion of "position play." For now, as we approach stroke control, bear in mind the necessity of predetermining cue-ball action after it strikes the object-ball target.

Chalk Up Before Every Shot: There you are, already in your stance, and now I'm asking you to stand up and perform a quick but vital preliminary.

Apply chalk lightly to the cue tip, now and before every stroke, to avoid miscues—the "dub shots" of billiards.

Cue tips are made of leather or composition material whose texture does not provide friction sufficient to assure firm contact with the polished cue ball. And because the tip will come in contact with a ball (no flat surfaces), it needs the increased friction of chalk to avoid slipping off the intended point of contact.

Turn the chalk, never the cue, in a light back-and-forth motion or half-turn to deposit a light film of chalk on the cue tip before each shot.

This fact becomes even more important as you progress into shotmaking that calls for stroking the ball at points off dead center.

Here's the proper way of applying chalk to the cue tip; again, the emphasis is on "lightly." Don't turn the cue; turn the chalk in application. One light back-and-forth motion or half-turn, forward and back, is enough to deposit a light film of chalk on the tip. Chalk should never be applied so that it builds up a layer or flakes. Excessive chalk on the tip defeats its purpose.

Use a Short Stroke: Now return to your stance, facing the shot with your feet turned slightly to the right. Your grip with three fingers and thumb is three to six inches behind the cue's balance point, and you have formed a steady finger bridge to guide the shaft.

About eight inches of cue shaft should extend from your bridge channel to the cue ball. Short stroking action provides better control, and in this position your backstroke will be no longer than four to six inches.

The spring action of your arm and wrist will provide the amount of power needed to send the cue ball anywhere on the table. A longer stroke only increases the chance of off-target contact of cue tip and cue ball.

Warm-up Stroking: Golfers "waggle" a club before hitting, and baseball players take practice swings as they await a pitch. They do it to relax and loosen up in preparation for positive action. In our sport of billiards, we use warm-up stroking for the same purpose.

No more than eight inches of cue shaft should extend from your bridge to the cue ball as you prepare to shoot.

Two or three smooth practice strokes of the cue will keep your arm and wrist, loose before you stroke the ball.

The use of three or four rhythmic warm-up strokes before stroking the cue ball will serve to loosen your arm and wrist, and center your concentration upon the shot at hand.

At this point you have selected the object ball and surveyed the table to determine position for the next shot. In addition to helping you relax, the warm-up movements will aid you in "grooving" the stroke toward the intended point of contact with the ball.

Just don't get reckless in your preliminary stroking. Any accidental contact of cue and ball is a foul.

Stroke and Speed: If there was a sure-fire formula for perfect stroke control and speed, every billiard player would be an unbeatable champion and our sport would face extinction for lack of challenge.

The fact is, all billiard shots present challenges, and in infinite variety. You must plan and aim every stroke to pocket an intended object ball (with some strategy exceptions) and to send the cue ball into the best possible position for the next shot.

Don't shy from words like acquired "feel" and "sense" of stroking. They are the most expressive I can think of to describe the necessary ingredients to improve ability. The "feel" a good player develops for each stroke situation is the result of practice and concentration, and is only slightly related to natural talent.

The key words in billiard shotmaking are "soft" and "softer." Properly installed billiard tables are as level and true as man can make them. The balls are perfectly round, and this combination means that little force is needed to set the balls in motion and keep them rolling to desired positions.

Illustrate this to yourself by noting how little force is required to stroke the ball from near the head rail to the foot rail and back, as you will in "lagging" to determine the first shooter to start a game; or how a "soft" stroke can send the ball around the table, striking all four cushions.

These are only tests of speed. A later chapter on practice techniques will concentrate on gauging speed of stroke to help you develop the "feel" required to improve your ability.

Though it may sound a little like a dance step, here's the tempo of a billiard stroke—short, level, smooth, and soft.

Stroke "Through" the Ball: Good golfers and baseball players who make use of practice swings also know the value of follow-through—that smooth flow of action after the ball is hit. Neither I nor anyone else can tell you that the action you take after you hit the ball will affect its line of travel. After impact, there's nothing you can do to change your shot.

But it is as true in billiards as in any other sport that follow-through is pertinent to the entire action, and is very important in smoothing out the stroke motion and putting a finishing touch to the shot.

Your determination to follow through is a guarantee against jabbing or poking the ball, which are results of jerking the stroke up short. In billiards, a "jerk" is defined either as an impolite player or as an incomplete—and very likely unsuccessful—stroke.

Stroke short, level, smooth, soft, and "through" the ball. A proper follow-through will send your cue straight through the area occupied by the cue ball before it was hit. As you stroke

Follow-through is important in a billiard stroke. Note how the cue is sent through the area occupied by the cue ball before it was hit.

through the ball, your right elbow will drop slightly and your grip hand should pivot backward at the wrist to keep the cue traveling on a level plane.

If you started a backstroke with eight inches of cue shaft from finger bridge to cue ball, there should be twelve inches extended after follow-through. Infrequent exceptions will be necessary when shooting with an elevated cue or into a close ball cluster.

Start now to make full follow-through a part of each stroke. If you must, exaggerate it to form the habit. With practice, your follow-through will become as natural as forming a bridge.

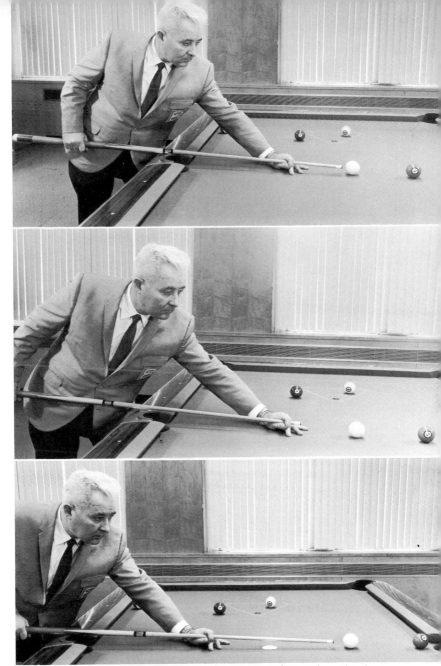

This photo sequence, from top to bottom, illustrates complete stroke action from aim to follow-through. Observe that my head is steady and that the cue remains level.

Get on the Ball

Stop, Follow, and Draw Shots

THE "moment of truth" in billiards is that split-second when cue tip meets cue ball and sets in motion the shot you have planned. All your preparation—grip, stance, bridge, and aim—are focused at moving the cue ball in a precise path required to hit and send the object ball into a pocket.

With the cue ball in motion, all you can do is watch—and hope. Assuming you have learned earlier lessons well, your chances for a successful shot are good. The *ker-thunk* of a pocketed object ball is a gratifying sound.

But we have indicated in previous chapters that playing to win requires execution of a series of successful shots. The object of most games of pocket billiards is to pocket in succession as many balls as possible before you relinquish the table to your opponent after a miss, foul, or in defensive strategy.

This calls for playing position—stroking the cue ball so that it not only drives the desired object ball into a pocket but also rolls into the best possible position for the next shot. Control of the cue ball can make you a winner.

Center-Ball Stroking: The vast majority of shots can, and should, be executed by stroking the cue ball at its exact center. At this point of cue-ball contact, you have the surest control of its line of roll to the object ball.

To strike the cue ball at dead center, use a standard bridge with normal finger elevation to bring the cue tip in line with the ball's center spot. With the cue level, stroke smoothly with full follow-through.

These overhead and rear views illustrate a center-ball stroke. A standard bridge is used to produce dead-center cue impact.

Properly stroked, the center-ball shot will stop the cue ball after its impact with an object ball. This will be true only when the shot calls for reasonably full impact with the object ball. When you "cut" the object ball—hit it to angle sharply—the cue ball may also angle away, even in a center-ball shot.

Nevertheless, the stop shot will be a valuable technique in many situations in which you want the cue ball to remain in the same relative position from which you moved the object ball.

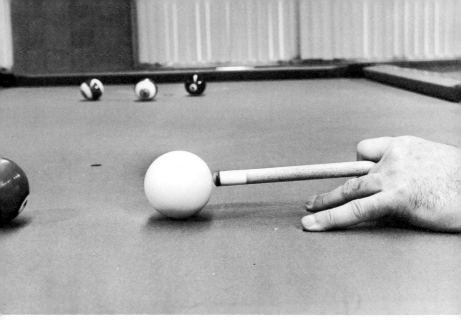

Here is a side view of cue position for a center-ball shot.

Follow Shot: Now comes our first variation in stroke to provide cue-ball control. It's called the follow shot simply because its execution sends the cue ball in the same general direction as the struck object ball.

Let's assume that you are shooting a ball into a corner pocket from a cue-ball position near the center of the table and that the next object ball in your sequence of strategy lies near the foot rail. A stop shot in this situation would leave the cue ball too far away and at a difficult angle from the next object ball.

A follow shot is the answer, and here's how to stroke it.

First of all, let me explain that the cut ball will "follow" only through the action of overspin. And to impart overspin to the cue ball, you must stroke it above center.

Remember what we've said about the value of keeping the cue level on all shots with very few exceptions? You can adhere to this rule and still stroke the follow shot. The solution is in your fingers.

As diagramed here, a center-ball stroke produces a stop shot, which keeps the cue ball near the position occupied by the object ball before impact.

Execute the follow shot by striking the cue ball a cue-tip width above center. Don't lower the butt of the cue to bring its tip into this position. This throws the cue off level and increases the danger of a miscue. To bring the cue tip into position for a follow stroke, elevate the bridge hand. Accomplish this by pulling your fingertips closer to your hand, forming a higher arch and cue channel. This bridge position elevates the cue tip to a follow-stroke impact level.

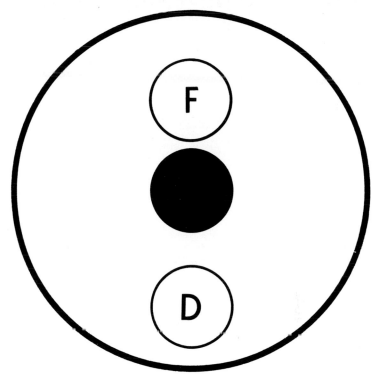

To produce a follow shot, strike the cue ball a cue-tip width above center. For a draw shot, the ball must be struck as far below center as possible, with the cue relatively level.

The follow-stroke bridge is illustrated from various angles in this chapter.

Take care to strike the ball only a cue-tip width above center, not higher, and follow through normally. And did you remember to chalk up before the shot? A properly chalked cue tip is vital to sure stroking of a follow shot.

Draw Shot: In practicing the follow shot, it doesn't take long to discover that this stroke is not the total solution to position play. In many situations the follow shot is plainly out of the question because it would send the cue ball away from the next object ball or, worse, into the pocket for a "scratch." When you scratch—pocket the cue ball—any object ball pocketed in the same shot must be returned to the table, and your opponent takes over.

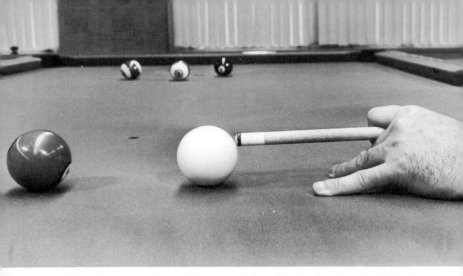

Bring the cue tip into position for a follow shot by elevating the bridge hand. Accomplish this by pulling your fingertips closer to your hand, forming a higher arch and cue channel.

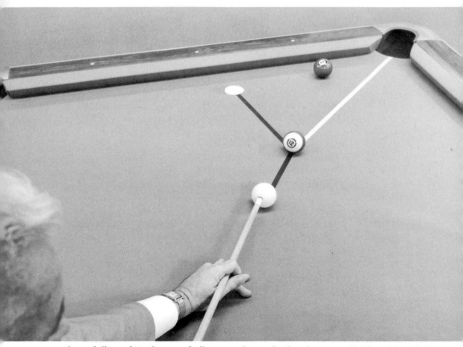

In a follow shot the cue ball moves forward after impact with the object ball. In this illustration the cue ball veers left because the object ball had to be angled to the right to be pocketed.

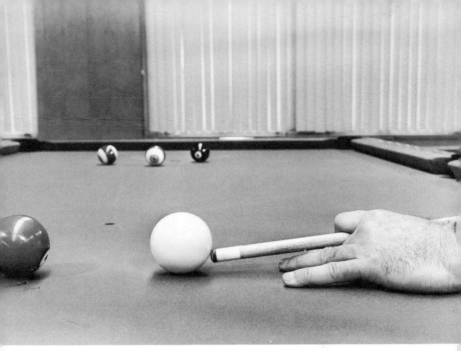

By extending and spreading the fingers of your bridge hand, you will lower the cue tip into position for a draw shot.

A stop shot should be your choice to avoid scratching in some situations. In others, in which you want the cue ball to roll backward from its object-ball impact, use the draw shot. "Draw" is the reverse of "follow," and means that you give the cue ball underspin to reverse its direction after impact with an object ball.

You're right. To apply draw to the cue ball, strike it below center—as low as possible with a level cue. The diagram in this chapter illustrates cue-ball impact points for center-ball, follow, and draw strokes. You will note that the draw shot calls for cue-tip impact at a point lower than a cue-tip width below center. A low impact point is required to give the ball decisive draw action.

You're right again. Lower the bridge—don't elevate the cue butt—to bring the cue tip into position for a draw shot. By extending and spreading the fingers of your bridge hand, you will lower the cue tip without altering levelness of the cue.

As in the case with follow shots, some draw-shot situations will require the use of other than a basic bridge. One such situation is pictured here to guide you. The butt end of the cue must be raised higher than normal to put the cue tip in draw-shot position with a rail or vee bridge.

You can't spend practice time any better than in mastering center-ball, follow, and draw strokes. They form the stock-in-trade of a good billiard player—one who exercises maximum cue-ball control with a minimum of fancy maneuvers.

Draw action on the cue ball pulls it back from impact with an object ball and into position for the next shot, as shown here.

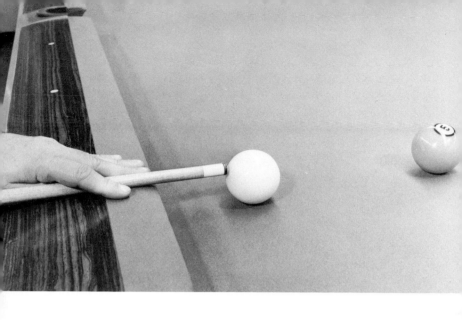

From close to the rail, a follow shot (top photograph) or draw shot (lower photograph) can be executed with a normal rail bridge.

A Useful Twist

Application of English

BEGINNING pocket-billiard players would be well advised to skip concentration and practice on this lesson for the present. As a beginner, you can return to this section after your basic shotmaking sharpens a bit.

But since this book is intended to help beginners and advanced players alike, it is necessary at this point to include a brief chapter on "how" and "why" to apply English to the cue ball. Serious students of the game must develop a stroke for English and an awareness of its value in certain shot and position play situations.

Don't let English scare you. I stress the advanced nature of this stroke technique only because of its special applications. Center-ball, draw, and follow shots generally will carry you around the table with successful shots and good cue-ball position. Resort to English only when you are confronted with the need to alter cue- or object-ball action radically.

What is "English"? Don't ask me the origin of the word in this sense. I must defer to other specialists for an explanation of how "English" came to define unusual spin on a ball—billiard or otherwise. (Some say it comes from "Angle," but I don't know.) English is the application of abnormal spin on a ball that can alter its course before and after it strikes an object. Ball spin produces a curve on a baseball and hooking action on a bowling ball. Now let's close the "Mosconi School of Physics" and consider the practical application of English to the playing of billiards.

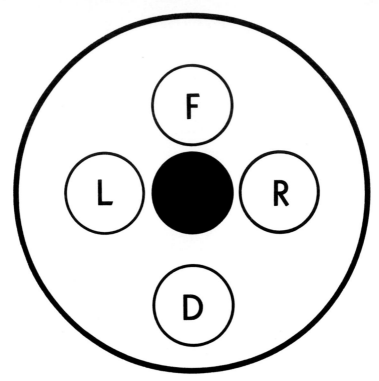

Right or left English can be applied to the cue ball by striking it no more than a cue-tip width to the right or left of center.

You've already learned that more than normal overspin on the cue ball—applied by stroking it above center—will produce a follow shot. And by stroking the ball below center, you can draw it back from object-ball impact with draw-shot underspin. English is an extension of these techniques, and produces either clockwise or counterclockwise spin on the cue ball, depending on where it is stroked.

Stroke for English: You can apply all the English ever required on the cue ball by stroking it no more than a cue-tip width to the right or left of center. As we pointed out on the follow shot, cue-tip impact farther than cue-tip width from center increases the likelihood of a miscue.

To stroke for English, use a standard bridge with the fingers of the bridge hand extended normally, as they are for a center-ball shot. The difference, of course, is that you will position the bridge hand to bring the cue tip in line with a point of intended impact right or left of center.

With the cue tip chalked, take several warm-up strokes; then stroke firm and sharp with full follow-through.

How English Affects the Cue Ball: Our description of English said that it affects ball action both before and after it strikes an object. This is the fact that makes proper control of English a bit complicated. In billiards, English alters the path of the cue ball to the object ball and changes cue-ball reaction after it strikes a cushion. English also affects the direction of a struck object ball, but we shall elaborate on that later.

Here's a player's-eye view of cue position to produce right English.

Left English.

Application of English will cause the cue ball to curve in the direction of the English, left or right. The amount of curve increases with the length of the shot.

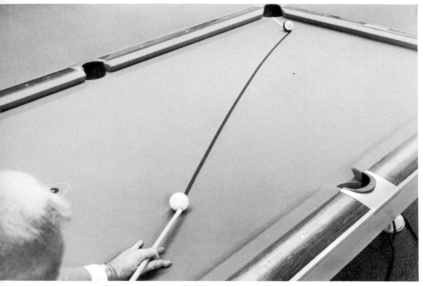

By striking the cue ball to the right of center, you produce counterclockwise spin and therefore right English. Stroked right, the cue ball tends to curve right, with the amount of curve increasing with the length of the shot. You can see now why the application of English is a trifle tricky. In aiming a long shot with English, you must compensate for the curve of the cue ball as you aim its point of impact with the object ball.

Right English also adds speed to the cue ball, and widens its angle of deflection after it strikes a cushion, at least in straightforward shots to a cushion. In a difficult shot situation, these can be important factors in positioning the cue ball.

This cue-ball action—its path to an object ball, speed, and deflection angle off a cushion—is reversed when it is struck left of center. Left English sends the cue ball curving to the left, and again this principle applies: The longer the shot, the greater the curve. It also decreases the speed of the cue ball and narrows its angle after striking a cushion. The accompanying table diagram will, I hope, clear away any confusion resulting from this quick cadence of "rights" and "lefts."

This piece of advice bears repeating. English can be a useful, and on some occasions a necessary, stroke technique in your game strategy. It's well worth practicing, but only at a point in the development of your ability when you feel confident enough to move into this phase of advanced shotmaking.

English affects the angle of cue-ball rebound after it strikes a cushion. The angle narrows as a result of right English, outlined here in white. The dark line illustrates the wider angle produced by left English. The effect would be reversed on banks to the cushion from the opposite angle.

In the Pocket

Hit the Object Ball, and Score

UP to now, we've directed our attention—and yours, we hope—to the necessary preliminaries to pocket-billiards play. Concentration on grip, stance, bridge, and stroke comprises the vital sequence of steps leading to movement and control of the cue ball.

Obviously, you can't play the game, much less win, by merely shoving the cue ball around the table. The cue ball must hit object balls within narrow limits of precision, sending them into designated pockets. What happens to the cue ball after it sends an object ball to a pocket is the key to setting up the next shot to start building what we call a "run," or series, of successful shots. High runs are the big thrills in billiards, and the ingredients of victory.

For now, however, let's concentrate on one object ball at a time.

It is time now to reopen the "Mosconi School of Applied Science." This lecture will be blessedly brief, and it never hurts any of us to think through the "why" of something. It's worth examining what happens when the cue ball strikes the object ball.

When the cue ball is stroked to give it either straightforward or reverse roll over its horizontal axis—follow, stop, or draw shot—it will move a struck-object ball at an angle equal to the angle of impact axis on the cue ball. There's a mouthful for you. While you're scratching your head, wondering why Mosconi doesn't switch to engineering, let me describe a simple experiment you can, and should, try.

Helpful Experiment: With chalk or a crayon, draw a line over the top and down the sides of an object ball in the direction of the intended pocket. Now draw a line on the cue

Here is the experiment in aiming described in the text. In this case, tape is used to indicate contact points both on cue and on object balls. By moving the cue ball along its intended path to where the tapes meet (lower photograph), you can illustrate to yourself what part of the cue ball you should have aimed to make this shot.

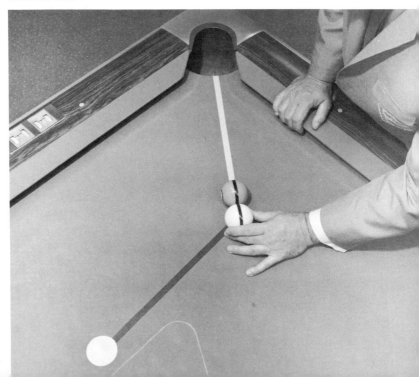

ball that, if extended to the cushion, would be parallel to the line from object ball to pocket. Now place the cue ball in contact with the object ball, matching up the lines on both. The point of impact necessary to pocket the ball is the point at which the lines touch.

Before the purists howl, I hasten to add that this simple experiment (illustrated in this chapter) does not take into account an allowable margin for impact error, and most certainly does not apply when English (sideways spin) is applied to the cue ball.

For the moment, though, I hope this little exercise will help you grasp the principle of object-ball reaction. I've seen intense players study a shot, then apply chalk from their cue tip to the intended impact point on both cue ball and object ball. This sort of help in aiming would not be permitted in a match, but I see nothing wrong with it as a practice device. Just don't become dependent on it.

Which brings us to the main point of this chapter—to help you to develop an "eye" for sighting the object ball, aiming the cue ball, and to outline special strokes for certain advanced shotmaking.

Sighting: Who says the playing of pocket billiards does not involve exercise? Aside from bending into a stance, which is good for most waistlines, there is considerable walking in our game. Some observers comment that I seem to circle the table more often than many other players during the course of a match. If I do, it's not only because I need the exercise; I also "stalk" the table to sight my shots.

It will not be necessary for you to walk around the table to line up each shot. Some will be relatively simple to plan and execute. Others, requiring a sharp angle of attack, should be surveyed from the direction of the intended pocket and from the point of impact. Such multiple sighting will serve to train your judgment in sizing up the shot at hand and others to follow.

As you survey a shot from several angles, I hope you remember our experiment. If you extend an imaginary line from the pocket through the object ball, it will emerge at the required point of contact. This point of contact remains the same regardless of cue-ball position.

73

Earlier, we mentioned an allowable margin of error. This means, simply, that the point of contact is considerably larger than a pinhead. You must realize that a corner-pocket opening is about 5 inches wide and that object balls are 2¼ inches in diameter. In other words, you can fit two object balls in a pocket opening, and then some. Feel better? Well, don't relax too much. As the length of the shot increases, the margin for error decreases. Our game is still one of precision.

Sighting, then, is a matter of determining the point of contact on an object ball. Once you have, you must retain this mental picture and prepare to send the cue ball on a path to establish contact.

Aiming: Remember our emphasis on stance in which you were positioned to bring your head directly in line with the cue? If you've ever shot a rifle, you know why.

Aiming a billiard shot is comparable to aiming a rifle in all respects except for the fact that your cheek is not against the cue as it would be against the rifle stock. There are two points

This illustration duplicates how you should visualize and aim this shot. Your line of aim should extend from the right side of the cue ball to the edge of the object ball.

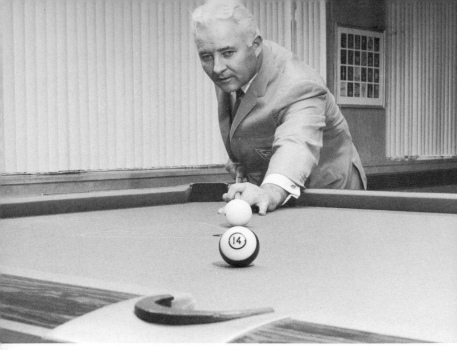

Note that in aiming a shot, my head is directly above the cue and my eyes are on the object ball during the stroke.

of reference in aiming a billiard shot—the contact points on both cue ball and object ball. In rifle shooting, your eye follows the line from sight groove to the target.

Just beware of carrying the analogy to an extreme. The exact center of a cue ball can never be the contact point. This point always is somewhere on the curved, outside edge of the ball, and that's where your line of sight should carry to the surface point on the object ball. Only in straightaway shots—those with no angle to the pocket involved—will you be aiming across the center of the cue ball.

In answer to a frequent question about aiming, I can assure you that I always keep my eyes on the object ball during a stroke. Preliminary to this, I have positioned my body and bridge hand to bring the cue tip in line with where I intend to hit the cue ball. I shift my eyes from cue ball to object ball and make any minor adjustments in cue position necessary, much as a golfer glances from ball to hole in putting,

76

except that no head movement is required in billiard aiming.

From the time I start the cue back until the follow-through is completed, my eyes are glued to the object-ball contact point. Then I watch the ball disappear into the pocket—most of the time.

Before we complicate things a bit, it might be well to insert a word here about confidence. Practice is the only sure foundation for successful shotmaking, and success breeds confidence. While you're about your practice, think success. Golf instructors often tell their students to think of the hole as if it were a bushel basket. Remind yourself as a billiard student that the pocket is more than two balls wide and an accessible target from anywhere on the table. Self-assurance in your ability to sight, aim, and execute a variety of shots is basic to improvement.

Effects of English: In our chapter on English, we outlined in some detail the effect of right or left sideways spin on the cue ball. You will recall that when the cue ball is stroked to the right of center, it curves right as a result of counterclockwise spin. English left, applied by stroking the ball to the left of center, forces the ball to curve left. The amount of curve increases with the length of the shot, and a soft stroke will produce more curve than a hard one.

When a cue ball stroked for English contacts an object ball, there is a transfer of the English effect—in the opposite direction. This produces what we call a "throw" shot simply because the effect is to throw the object ball away from the direct path it would follow if it were hit by a center-stroked cue ball.

Just remember that an object ball hit with cue-ball English left will be thrown right. It would be thrown left when struck by a cue ball stroked for English right.

Throw shots are useful when you face extra-thin cuts on the object ball and when you want the cue ball to alter its course after contact. You must compensate for the throw effect of English in aiming at the object ball. Knowing that English right on the cue ball throws the object ball left, the object-ball contact point will be further left than normal.

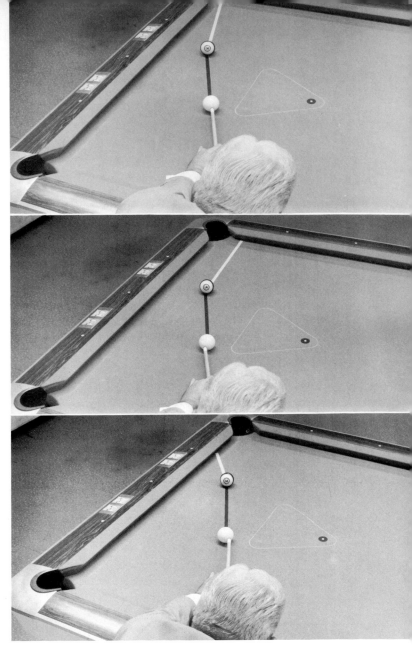

From top to bottom, we see the effect of stroking the cue ball center, English left, and English right. English left (middle photograph) throws the object ball to the right. English right (bottom photograph) throws the object ball to the left. You must compensate for this throw effect when you aim and shoot and apply English.

78

At this angle, an object ball resting against the cushion can be pocketed with a center stroke on the cue ball aimed to hit the cushion and object ball simultaneously.

Here's an example of when and how to use English. When an object ball is resting against a cushion, the normal shot called for is a center-ball stroke aimed to hit cushion and ball at the same time. This keeps the object ball from bouncing away from the cushion. This standard shot at a cushioned ball will not work if the angle requires too thin a hit by the cue ball. The alternative is to drive the cue ball to the cushion slightly behind the object ball and apply English in a direction that will transfer to the object ball and force it to hug the cushion on the way to a pocket.

Combination, Carom, and Bank Shots: One of the many rewards of your increasing skill at billiards will be your ability to recognize shot opportunities where, to the less practiced eye, apparently none exist. Billiard balls have an unpredictable way of clustering in every conceivable formation. In all but a very few situations, some sort of shot possibility exists. It's up to you to muster all your sighting skill to find it.

When a very thin hit is required on a cushioned ball, aim the cue ball to hit the cushion slightly behind the object ball, and apply English, in this case right-hand. This will produce a throw-left effect on the object ball, forcing it to hug the cushion on its way to the pocket.

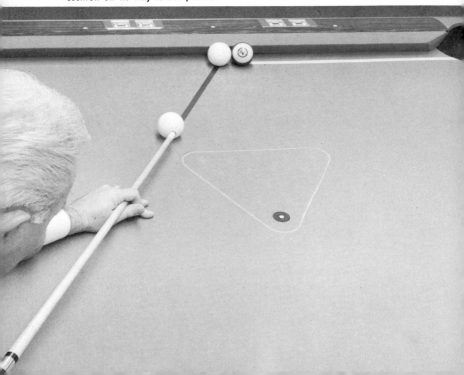

During a championship match, I may play safe and not attempt a highly complicated shot to avoid the risk of missing and opening up the cluster for my opponent. But during your friendly games, I urge you to study the table and try for a tough shot to gain the experience.

One fascinating challenge is the combination shot, one in which two or more balls must be set in motion to drive the called ball to a pocket. It's like a chain reaction.

The common expression is to refer to a combination as "on" if it appears that a proper sequence of throw actions on intervening balls will ultimately send the called ball in the right direction. When this appears impossible, the combination is "not on."

The two-ball combination at the left is "on," while the somewhat different arrangement at the right is "not on." In the "on" combination, stroke to produce the equivalent of English left on the 5-ball. This motion reverses itself in transferring to the called ball, 14, which is thrown right and into the pocket. The combination at right is "not on" because the 14-ball cannot be thrown far enough right to reach the pocket.

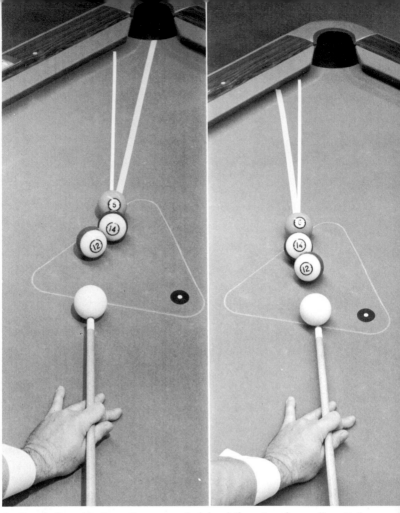

In three-ball combinations, the same principle of throw transfer applies. At the left, the shot is "on," and the 5-ball can be pocketed by throwing it to the right. A full hit on the 12-ball will start the necessary chain reaction. The combination at the right cannot be made because the called ball will be thrown left however the 12-ball is hit.

Illustrations in this chapter show examples of combinations that are "on" and "not on."

How do you determine this business of "on" and "not on"? First, examine the combination to make sure the balls are "frozen," or nearly so. Balls in "on" combinations must be touching or not more than one-eighth of an inch apart to sustain the transfer action. Next, determine the direction of

These four-ball combinations are arranged to illustrate when the called ball can be thrown into the pocket (photograph at the left) and when it cannot, as in the lineup at the right.

throw required on the called ball and work back toward the cue ball to decide if the combination of throw effects on each intervening ball will result in the desired action on the ball to be pocketed.

This is the chain reaction we mentioned in which you must use your understanding that the effect of throw reverses itself from ball to ball. When you practice, start by setting up two-ball combinations, and progress to three-, four-, and five-ball arrangements. Try shots that you are sure are "on," and arrange others that are not to help develop your sighting sense.

Carom shots differ from combinations in that the cue ball hits a called ball that must deflect, or carom, off one or more other object balls to be pocketed. You can make carom shots when the balls are farther apart than is possible in combinations.

When the called ball in a carom is frozen to another object ball, an imaginary line drawn from the pocket must extend directly in between the balls to permit use of a center-ball stroke. Let's assume the balls are frozen but not in line with a pocket. A draw shot on the cue ball will produce overspin (follow) on the called ball and force both balls toward the pocket line while the carom is taking place.

When two balls are touching, or nearly so, on this line to a pocket, call the 5-ball and hit it on the right side. It will carom off the 14, and score.

A special technique is required for this carom shot because a line from between the two balls does not extend to the pocket. To score the 5-ball, apply draw action to the cue ball. This produces overspin on the 5 and moves both balls to positions indicated by paper spots before the carom is completed.

This carom shot shows the path of the 5-ball, which is made to deflect off the 8-ball and into the pocket.

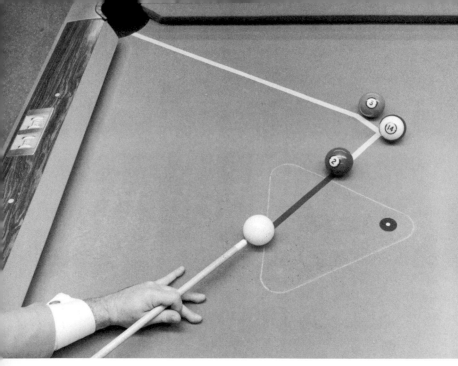

In this ball arrangement, the 2-ball can be made to carom off the 14- and 3-balls to give it a roundabout, but successful, path to the pocket.

This and other carom-shot situations are illustrated here to acquaint you with a variety of carom opportunities. And here's a pleasant thought: You just might, in the process of a carom shot, pocket both the called ball and another that was carom hit. A two-point stroke like this can rarely be planned, but it's within the rules as long as the called ball is scored.

Bank shots—when an object ball strikes one or more cushions on the way to a pocket—are difficult, even for the best of players. When the house trophy is at stake, attempt a bank shot only when you're satisfied no easier shot exists and when you choose not to play safe.

A ball's reaction off the cushion is difficult to predetermine, and most bank shots must be played at the more difficult side pockets. Bank shots must be stroked harder than normal, not only because of the distance involved but also to keep the ball from drifting away from the proper angle as it leaves the cushion.

Bank shots are part of the game, or else it wouldn't be necessary to have more than four markers spaced along the table rails. These spots are used to determine bank-shot angles. Here's how to use them. Draw an imaginary line from the object ball to the cushion; then determine how many dot spaces this is from the pocket. Divide by two, and you have arrived at the proper bank point on the cushion. Refer to the accompanying photo for a diagram of bank-shot angles.

Remember that English affects the ball's rebound angle from a cushion. English right on the cue ball produces what amounts to English left on the object ball. The reverse is true, of course, for English left.

There you have all you need to know—on paper at least—to sight, aim, and pocket the object ball. Really to learn what you've read, play the game every chance you get. Take advantage of help from a qualified instructor, and practice, always realizing that pocket billiards is a game of judgment built on experience.

This photograph illustrates our explanation of bank shot angles. Because the 3-ball is two rail markers above the pocket, it should be aimed through the cushion at the first marker. The 14-ball, located one and one-half markers from the pocket, must be banked halfway, or a distance three-quarters of the first marker space from the pocket.

Sharpen Your Stroke

Practice Drills for All Players

BEING close doesn't count in our game, but billiards and horseshoes are alike in one respect—you can enjoy and learn a lot about both by playing alone. Nothing can replace the excitement of a challenging match against an opponent of equal ability, but for purposes of practice you should spend some time alone at the table, getting and keeping your stroke sharp.

In this chapter I outline and illustrate several practice drills designed to help you progress from beginner to winner. They can take you a long way toward increasing your skill in four basic elements of billiard play:

1. Stroke speed
2. Effects of follow, draw, and English
3. Position play
4. Advanced shotmaking

Before you launch into a practice session, check your grip, stance, and bridge against the recommendations in earlier chapters. Practicing bad habits is worse than not practicing at all. I've watched too many otherwise promising players reach a certain level of skill, then falter and fail to progress further. Usually, this failing is a matter of simple faults in the player's elementary technique. For instance, too tight a grip on the cue can hinder your development of proper stroke speed and follow-through.

Now let's practice—often. Here are some drills for use either in practice time or as warm-ups for a match.

Start simply, by spotting several balls at varying distances from side and corner pockets. Select a cue-ball spot and use

A random arrangement of balls like this provides a good warm-up exercise in center-ball stroking.

Try this series of long shots to corner pockets, using draw strokes to play position.

Playing position to pocket this series of balls clustered near a side pocket provides a test of your stroke speed.

If you can play this lineup of practice shots by controlling cue-ball movement, it means that your practice is paying off.

center-ball stroking at each object ball. Run through a series of shots, using a basic bridge; then move the cue-ball spot closer to the cushion and reshoot the series, using a rail bridge.

Try Long Shots: Bothered by the difficulty of long shots? You're not alone, and that's why even professional players try to avoid scattering the balls over the full length of the table. At times, long shots will be unavoidable, and when you face them, come equipped with experience gained in practice. Spot object balls near each corner pocket and play them the long way. Follow this drill by spotting several balls along the head string, and shoot for the corner pockets at the foot rail.

You can put your draw-shot skill to a test with this one. Arrange a semicircle·of balls near a side pocket. Start at either end and work your way left or right, pocketing a ball and drawing your cue ball back into position for the next shot. Stroke speed, as well as draw action, will be practiced in this setup.

Using a piece of paper to indicate cue-ball position after each shot, plan a run of balls leading to good break position. A follow stroke here will send the cue ball to the rail and out.

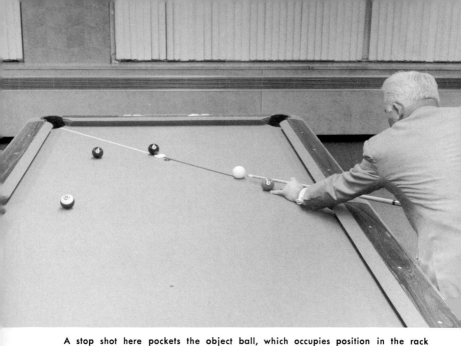

A stop shot here pockets the object ball, which occupies position in the rack area, and leaves the cue ball in line for a side-pocket shot.

Another stop shot here provides good cue-ball position to score the key ball.

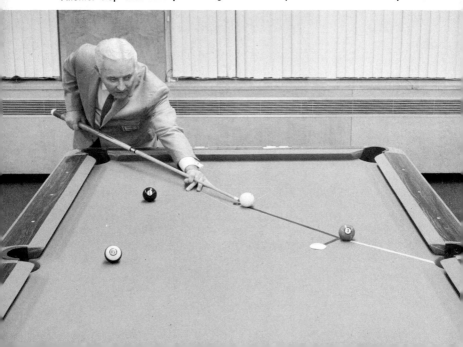

Now angle four balls or more down the length of the table, with the ball nearest you closer to the cushion. With the cue ball along the head string, stroke your way up the table with the idea in mind of playing the best possible cue-ball position for the succeeding shot.

Position Drill: To attain even more precision in playing position, use a piece of paper as a training device. Scatter a few balls on the table—I would advise less than the full 15 to avoid blocking pockets—and start calling your shots, two at a time. Before you shoot, spot the piece of paper at the desired cue-ball position for the next shot. You will be aiming both to pocket a ball and to bring the cue ball to rest on or near the paper.

While you're at it, go ahead and rack the balls for a game of 14.1 continuous or rotation billiards. Play yourself a match, but don't pull any shady stuff because you'll be watching. On second thought, why not reset the shots you miss and try again? It's only practice.

Again a stop shot is called for to pocket the key ball and position the cue ball at an angle that makes the break shot relatively easy

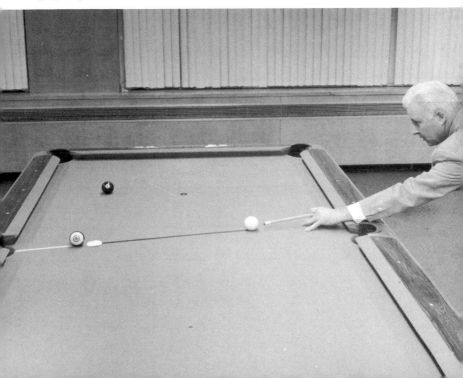

Now that you are flushed with victory in a match (against yourself), set up a few combination and carom shots like those illustrated in the previous chapter.

Contrary to the old adage, practice won't make you perfect. But it will bring you as close to perfection as ambition and talent will permit. And it's enjoyable.

Right-hand English on a follow shot against the break ball will send the cue ball into the rack and scatter the object balls sufficiently to keep your run intact.

Let's Play the Game

AS Shakespeare had Cleopatra say to one of her attendants, "Let's to billiards."

Having learned your lessons well, it is time now to tackle a game of 14.1 Continuous-Play Pocket Billiards. That's the full title of the game of 14.1, which is the common form of tournament and league competition. It is a demanding challenge to all the skills in pocket billiards, combining the strategy of offense and defense.

The term "14.1 Continuous Play" describes game procedure. Starting with the full rack of 15 balls, a player stays at the table until he misses. Balls are pocketed until one remains. The 14 pocketed balls then are reracked, and the game proceeds until one player reaches a predetermined point total, usually 125 or 150.

A digest of rules for 14.1 and other pocket-billiards games is printed elsewhere in this book. We shall discuss some of the rules here as they apply to the situations we outline.

Play to Win: On offense, your goal is to stay at the table as long as possible to build a "run" of successive points before you miss or purposely let your opponent take over as a defensive maneuver. Concentration on the following basic elements of offense can make you a winner:

—Play cue-ball position. This means controlling the cue ball so that it comes to rest at a spot you have determined best for the next shot. You should keep the cue ball away from the cushions. A cushioned cue ball limits your choice of stroke.

—Avoid long shots. This is another way of urging you to stroke soft, with just enough force to pocket the object ball and position the cue ball. Excessive stroke force can scatter object balls the full length of the table, creating more difficult shots.

97

Top players attempt to confine their shots to the upper half of the table from side pockets to foot rail.

—Break apart object-ball clusters. Part of your position play should involve spreading apart object balls that are clustered, and clearing the paths to pockets.

—Plan ahead. Keeping a run intact and assuring yourself of a good break shot against a new rack calls for planning shots well in advance. When you step to the table, survey the arrangement of balls to determine the best sequence of shots leading to the break.

How the Game Starts: Players "lag" to start a game. In the lag, each player shoots a cue ball from behind the head string to the foot rail and back to the head rail. The player whose ball rests closest to the head rail has the option of shooting first or forcing his opponent to do so.

The lag winner usually elects to have his opponent shoot first because it is unlikely that an object ball can be pocketed in a break shot against the 15-ball rack. In turn, the player who must shoot first usually plays safe on an opening break. To accomplish this without a two-point penalty, he must hit the rack of balls, driving two object balls and the cue ball to a cushion. Since playing safe on the opening is common strategy, it is worth practicing.

A standard form of opening break shot is illustrated in this chapter. With the cue ball "in hand," meaning I can position it anywhere behind the head string, I stroke for a thin hit on one of the corner balls in the rack. It and the opposite corner ball are forced to separate cushions and return to near their original position in the rack. The cue ball strikes three cushions and comes to rest near the head rail.

Since no ball was pocketed, my opponent takes over with his chances to score about as slim as mine were as the first shooter. Had I failed to send two object balls and the cue ball to a cushion, I would have been handed the two-point penalty and perhaps been forced to break again at my opponent's option.

Because my break shot was successful, my opponent can either shoot away by calling the ball he intends to pocket, or announce his intention to play a safety.

My favorite opening break shot produces a thin hit on a corner ball, sending it and the opposite corner ball to different cushions and back to the rack. The cue ball hits three cushions and comes to rest near the head rail. Executed properly, this break shot will force your opponent to play a safety.

Playing a safety requires hitting an object ball and driving it, or the cue ball, to a cushion. In this safety, I hit the corner ball very thin to avoid disturbing the rack, and return the cue ball to the head end of the table.

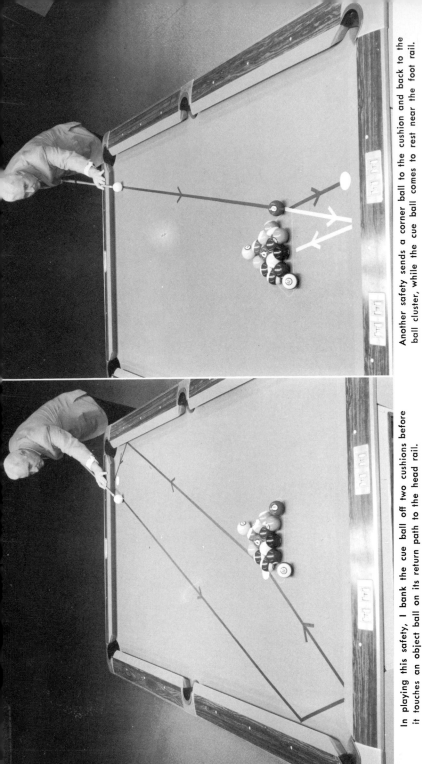

In playing this safety, I bank the cue ball off two cushions before it touches an object ball on its return path to the head rail.

Another safety sends a corner ball to the cushion and back to the ball cluster, while the cue ball comes to rest near the foot rail.

Safety Play: Safety play in billiards is like a football coach substituting his heavyweight linemen for a goal-line stand. Both are designed to keep opponents from scoring.

To execute a safety without a penalty, a player must drive an object ball to a cushion or drive the cue ball to a cushion after contact with an object ball. Failure at either alternative results in a scratch and a one-point penalty. You should play a safety anytime the object ball arrangement is such that no reasonable shot exists. Attempting, and missing, an extremely difficult shot can open up the balls and permit your opponent to shoot away with ease.

Illustrated here are several safety shots in which the balls were disturbed very little and the cue ball was returned to a position difficult for my opponent. This is the purpose of safety play. If I am forced to relinquish the table, I want my opponent to face a shot situation as tough as the one he left me.

Scratch Play: During the course of play in a tight match, a situation could develop in which you might intentionally stroke to relinquish the table and accept a one-point penalty. This is called "playing a scratch." To do so, you need only stroke the cue ball and intentionally fail to meet the requirements for a safety.

Here I play an intentional scratch and accept a 1-point penalty. I chose not to risk disturbing the pack, and banked the cue ball to the cluster, which will force my opponent also to play a defensive shot.

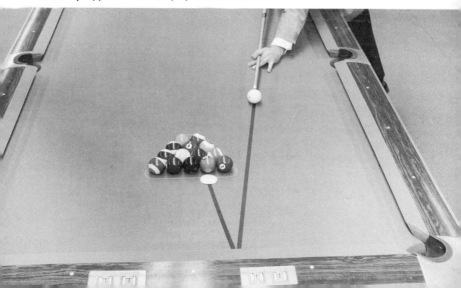

Unintentional scratches, when the cue ball enters a pocket or jumps off the table, also result in a one-point penalty, and give your opponent the next shot with the cue ball "in hand." Any object ball pocketed during a scratch is respotted on the table and is not scored.

Just beware of scratching, intentionally or accidentally, on three successive turns at the table. Three scratches, without an intervening point scored or safety, result in a 15-point penalty.

Play Position: Once the balls are spread sufficiently to permit shooting away, perhaps after a series of safeties, you can proceed to plan and execute a sequence of shots. Sight carefully to pocket an object ball, and move the cue ball with the follow, draw, or English action necessary to position it for the next shot. Remember the requirement to call your shots. You must announce to your opponent, or the referee, the number of the ball you intend to score and the pocket it will reach.

As you progress through a series of shots, you should be looking ahead to both the "key" ball and the "break" ball.

The key ball will be the next-to-last ball remaining on the table after pocketing the others. It is key because in scoring it you must attempt to send the cue ball to a position from where it will be possible both to score the break ball and scatter a new rack of 14 object balls.

Break Shot: To maintain a run of more than 14 balls—and practice will make this possible—you must pocket the break ball and drive the cue ball into the new rack with force sufficient to spread apart the cluster. While it's possible to scatter the rack from practically any break-ball and cue-ball position on the table, obviously some positions are better than others.

It's up to you in planning your shots to save as your break ball the one that appears best positioned for this purpose in relation to your intended cue-ball spot after pocketing the key ball. You will note in the illustrations that a pencil line is drawn around the ball-racking triangle to play 14.1. This is necessary to give the players an area of reference for selection of a break-ball and cue-ball position for the break.

If the final unpocketed ball is within the rack area, it must be placed on the head spot to permit the reracking of the other 14 balls. When both the cue ball and the final unpocketed ball

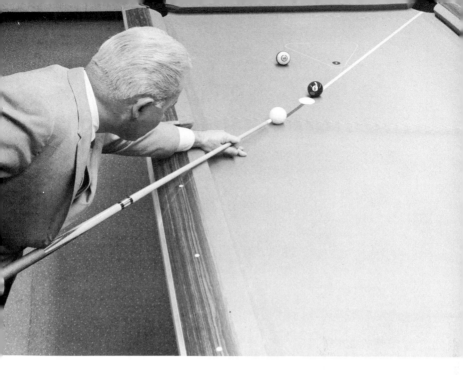

Playing the key ball to produce the best possible cue-ball position for the break is vital to extending a run. A stop shot (top photograph) or a follow shot (lower photograph) is necessary in these break-ball situations.

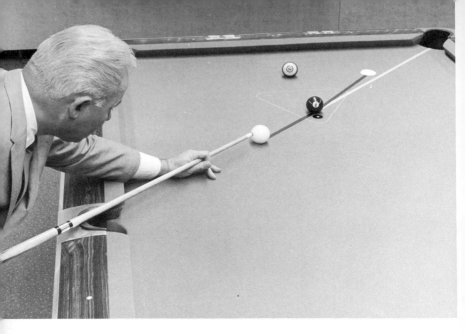

In the top photograph, the key ball is pocketed from within the rack area, and follow action on the cue ball sends it to good break position. Draw action is required in the lower photograph to draw the cue ball back from the key ball and into an easy angle for the break shot.

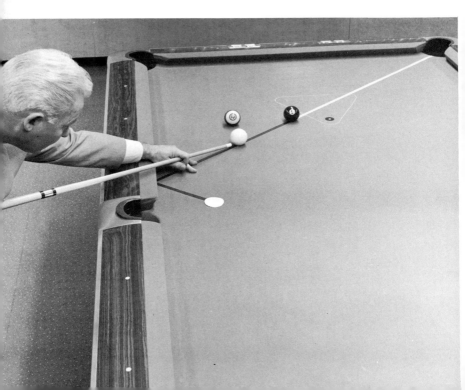

interfere with the rack, all 15 object balls are racked, and the player must shoot the cue ball from behind the head string.

When only the cue ball interferes with the rack, and the final object ball is above the head string, the 14 balls are racked as usual and the cue ball is "in hand" to be shot from behind the head string. In this situation, if the object ball is behind the head string, the cue ball must be shot from the head spot.

Now, play the game and may all your runs be long ones.

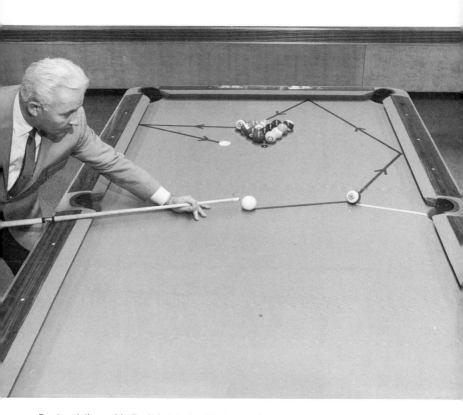

Employ follow with English left in this break shot to a side pocket. This shot is somewhat difficult because of the force required to send the cue ball to two cushions before it hits the racked balls.

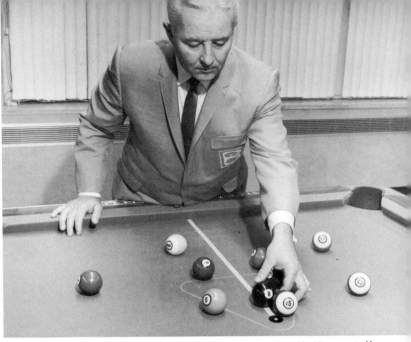

When object balls must be respotted, they must be placed on the foot spot. If the spot is blocked by another object ball, as it is here, the ball to be respotted must be placed behind the blocking ball and on a straight line from foot spot to foot rail.

This and the following seven photographs show break shots from various breakball and cue-ball positions. Follow action on the cue ball here will send it into the pack.

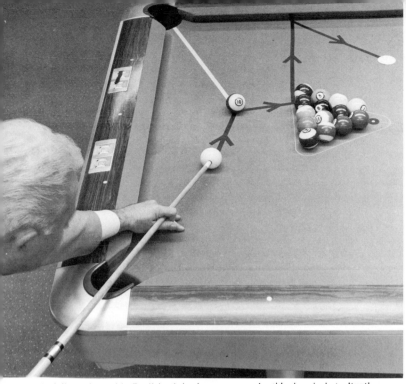

A follow shot with English right is necessary in this break-shot situation.

English left with follow against the break ball here will drive the cue ball into the pack and then away from the scattering balls.

Sharp draw action on the cue ball is required to pull it into the rack with enough force to open up the cluster.

Banking the cue ball after a thin hit on the break ball can open the cluster in this situation.

Follow with English left can open the rack from this difficult break-shot position.

English right will force the cue ball into the rack and then to a cushion while the balls separate.

Just for Fun

Learn to Perform Trick Shots

TRY this for a bit of home-style heroics. The next time you stroll into a billiard center or invite the neighbors to your home for a game, spot six balls in a cluster near the center of the table. Then, with as much nonchalance as you can muster, drive the cue ball into the cluster and relish the "oh's" and "ah's" from your spectators when each of the six balls plops home in a different pocket.

Sound impossible? Well, let me assure you it isn't. Any player of average ability who is willing to practice can learn to perform all the trick shots diagramed in this chapter—and many more.

I enjoy entertaining people by setting up and making a series of seemingly impossible shots. And it's always a highlight to select an unlikely shooter from the crowd and let him or her successfully make the shot I have arranged.

This illustrates the fact that ball placement is far more important than the stroke in a trick shot.

The late Charlie Peterson compiled what must have been the greatest repertoire of trick shots by challenging his audiences, "Show me a shot I can't make." To my knowledge, no one ever could.

I don't pretend to follow in Charlie's trick-shot footsteps. His sincere boast does point up the infinite variety of trick-shot possibilities, and for you, this means unlimited enjoyment. Some trial-and-error practice is required to master the shots described here and others you may develop. Be a trick-shot hero. That's part of the fun of our game.

"THE HUSTLER": Here's a shot I arranged for Jackie Gleason to make in the motion picture *The Hustler*. A center stroke on the blocked cue ball will set three balls in motion, forcing the called ball into a carom back to the upper right corner pocket.

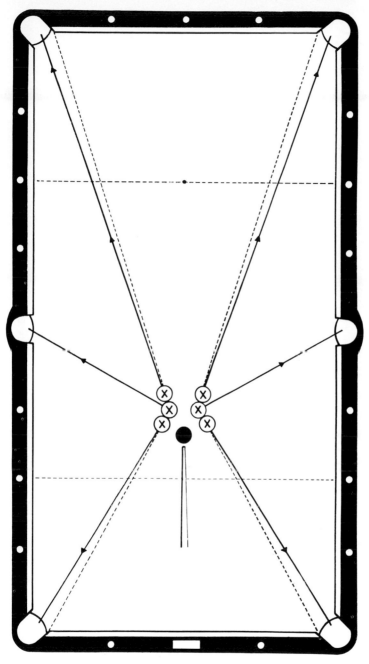

SIX BALLS—SIX POCKETS: The secret here is to aim the outside balls to the inside edge of the corner pockets as indicated by the dotted lines. Strike the cue ball (in black) hard and slightly below center.

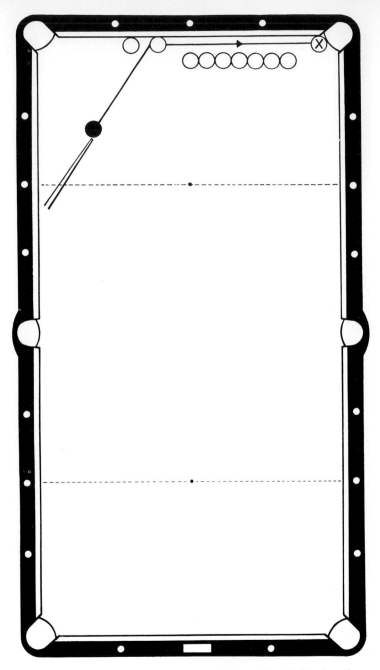

MACHINE GUN: Place the long string of balls in a line slightly less than a ball's width from the cushion. Strike the cue ball with high right English to force the struck object ball along the cushion. It will produce a "chatter" sound as it touches each ball in the lineup before pocketing the called ball, marked with an X.

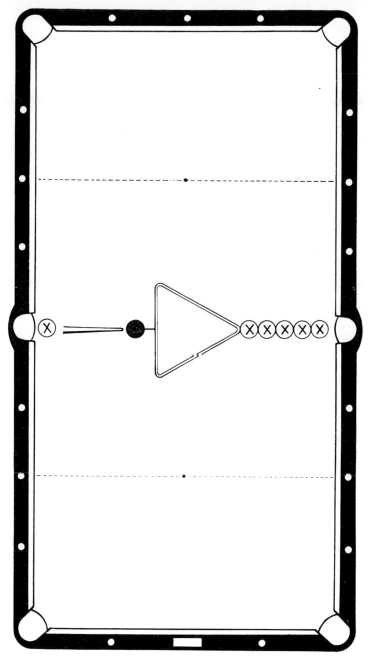

SIX BALLS—TWO POCKETS: Strike the cue ball with extreme draw. This will pull back the cue ball to pocket the single object ball after pushing the triangle against the other five, forcing them into the other side pocket.

AROUND THE RING: A center-ball shot here will bank the called ball off the cushion and into the corner pocket after it contacts each of the object balls set in a semicircle.

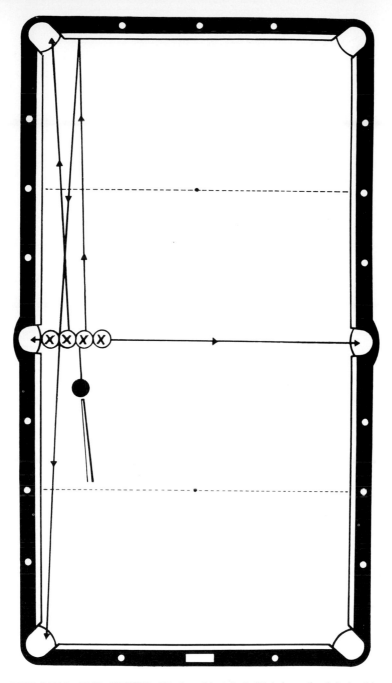

FOUR BALLS—FOUR POCKETS: Hit the object ball third from the left in this setup on the left side with a draw stroke on the cue ball. This keeps the cue ball out of the path of the third ball as it returns from the foot rail to the lower left corner pocket.

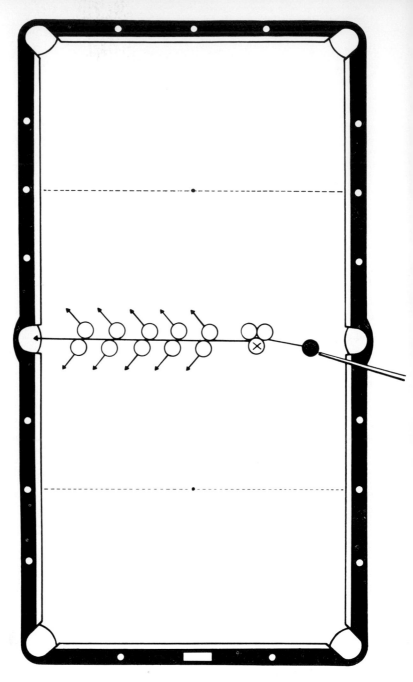

FOOTBALL SHOT: High left English on the cue ball in this arrangement will send the lower-right ball in the three-ball cluster through the 10-ball lineup like a "blocker" opening the path for the called ball.

SHARP BANK: Hit the cue ball sharply above center (follow stroke) to force the called ball off the cushion and into the opposite corner pocket. The cue must be lifted quickly after the stroke to avoid interfering with the banked ball.

JUMP THE RACK: A center hit on the cue ball against this cluster will send the called ball off the cushion and into the corner pocket by hitting the edge of the rack and jumping over the row of four balls. The rack must be wedged upright against the cushion.

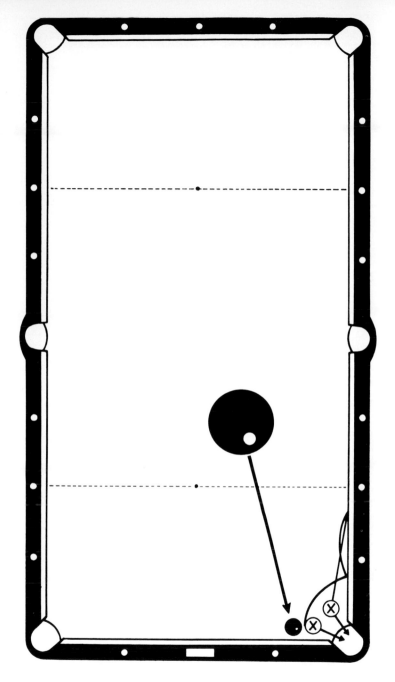

SHORT MASSE: Refer to the back cover of this book for an illustration of cue position for a massé shot. Strike the cue ball at the spot indicated in the enlarged view to produce radical backspin. The cue ball can be made to follow the black-line path to pocket both object balls. A word of warning: Missing the cue ball on this stroke can rip the cloth of the table.

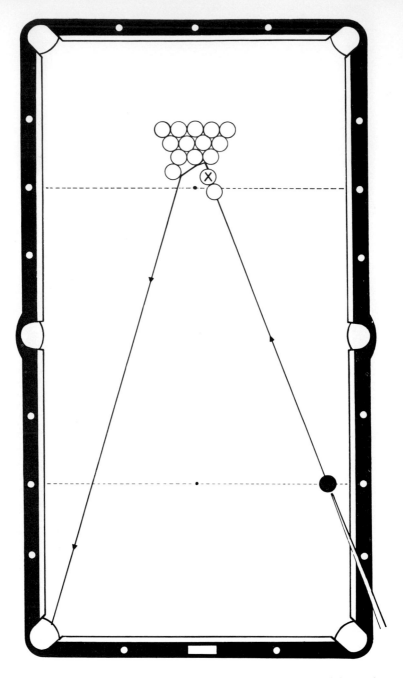

HANDKERCHIEF SHOT: Cover this ball arrangement with a handkerchief to make it look more difficult. A sharp center stroke on the cue ball will carom the called ball off three others in the pack and into the lower left corner pocket.

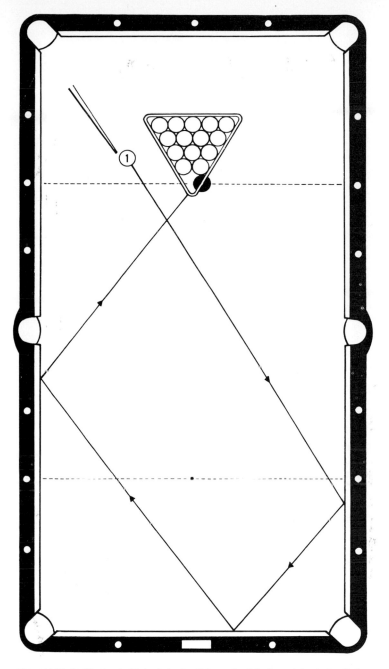

LAZY MAN'S RACK: Apply high right English to the 1-ball, and bank it off three cushions toward the foot spot. The ball will shove aside the cue ball on which the rack is resting, permitting the rack to drop to the table.

JUMP OUT: Elevate the butt end of the cue and strike the cue ball sharply above center. The cue ball can be made to jump over the edge of the rack, forcing the called ball to jump over the opposite edge of the rack and travel to the upper right corner pocket.

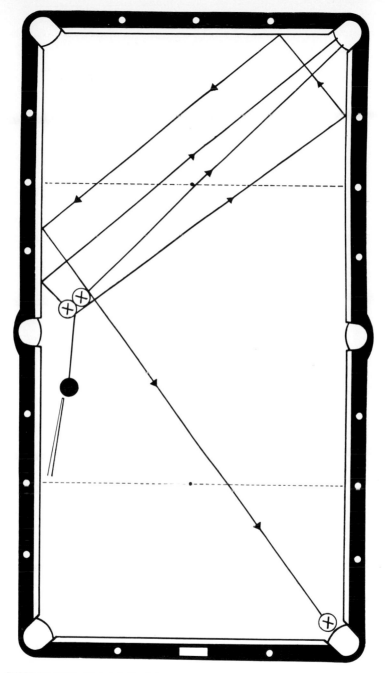

THREE IN ONE: High left English on the cue ball will drive two object balls to the upper right corner pocket. The cue ball then continues to bank off three cushions and return to pocket the third object ball positioned at the lower right corner pocket.

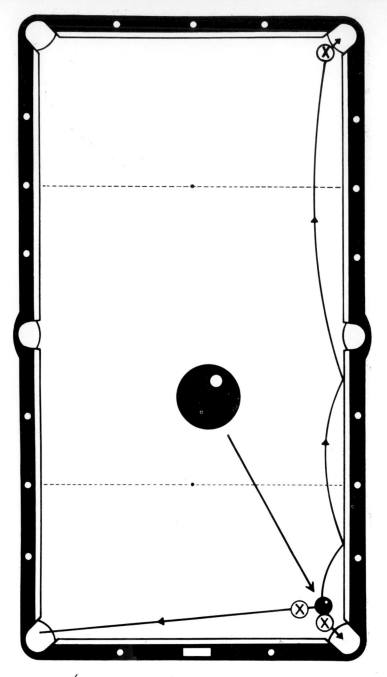

LONG MASSÉ: A massé stroke at the cue-ball spot indicated in the enlarged view can be made to pocket both balls at the head end of the table and travel along the side rail to pocket the ball at the upper right corner pocket.

BLOCKED CUE BALL: With the cue ball blocked behind the pocket opening, use a center stroke to bank off the side rail and into the cluster. The called ball, positioned as it is here, will carom into the upper right corner pocket.

UNDER THE BRIDGE: Position the mechanical bridge, two object balls, and the cue ball as shown here. Elevate the butt end of the cue and strike the cue ball sharply for a draw shot. This drives one object ball under the bridge to a pocket, and forces the cue ball to jump over the bridge and return to pocket the second object ball.

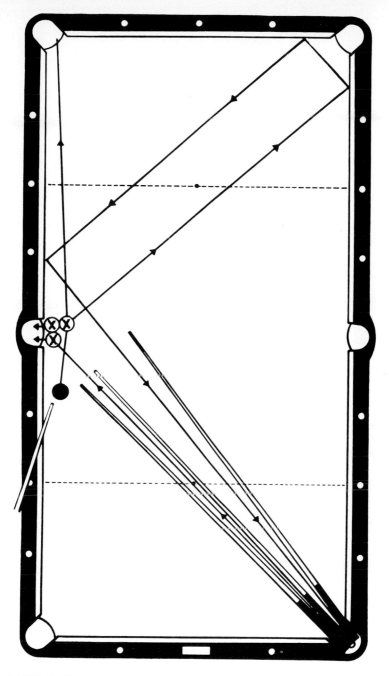

RAILROAD SHOT: Wedge three cues into a pocket for this shot. A high left-English stroke on the cue ball will drive two object balls to separate pockets and send the cue ball to three cushions before it travels up and down the cues to pocket the third object ball.

Talk a Good Game

BILLIARDS is an ancient sport, and through the centuries players have coined a collection of colorful terms to describe rules and situations of play. Much of the common vernacular of pocket billiards is given here in the hope that it will help increase your knowledge and appreciation of the game.

ANGLED: When the corner of a pocket prevents the player from shooting the cue ball in a straight line at an object ball.

BALL ON: When it can be shot at in a straight line or can be driven into a called pocket on a combination or carom shot.

BALLS STRUCK SIMULTANEOUSLY: It is permissible to strike balls simultaneously in call-shot pocket billiards if the player calls both ball and pocket.

BANK SHOT: Results when a player drives an object ball against a cushion and then into a pocket from that cushion.

BREAK: Opening shot of the game.

BRIDGE: The hand position as it holds and guides the cue shaft. It is also short for a mechanical bridge, a device used to make shots the player otherwise could not reach.

CALL SHOT: A requirement of some games that the player must make known his object ball and pocket intention before he shoots.

CALLED BALL: The ball a player announces he intends to score in a called pocket.

CALLED POCKET: The pocket into which a player announces he intends to drop a called ball.

CAROM: A shot in which the cue ball strikes each of two object balls; a rebounding, especially at an angle. *See also* KISS.

COMBINATION SHOT: A shot in which the cue ball sets in motion one or more intervening balls, with the last one striking the called object ball. A "chain reaction."

COUNT: A score—a point or number of points. In rotation, the number value of the ball pocketed.

CUE BALL IN HAND: When the player puts the ball in play at a point of his choice within the head string (*q.v.*).

CUSHION: The cloth-covered rubber ridge that borders the inside rails of the table.

CUT: To hit an object ball less than full at the center, causing the ball to deflect at an angle.

DEAD BALL: One that stops upon contact, the result of a stop shot.

DRAW: A stroking technique that allows the player to draw the cue ball back from an object ball.

ENGLISH: A stroking influence to control the action of the cue ball either before or after it hits an object ball. The result of ball spin.

FANCY SHOT: Usually an exhibition shot, a shot that requires unusual skill; a trick shot.

FEATHERING: To hit an object ball very thinly.

FOLLOW: A stroking technique that makes the cue ball roll in the same general direction as the struck object ball. Opposite of "draw."

FOOT SPOT: The spot for placement of object balls at the start of most games.

FORCE: The speed applied to the cue ball.

FORCE DRAW: The powerful application of "draw" to the cue ball, forcing the cue ball "through" the object ball before the cue ball begins to draw back, or drawing the cue ball back a great distance from the object ball.

FORCE FOLLOW: The firm application of follow that can drive the cue ball in a straight line "through" the object ball to a desired position.

FOUL: An infraction of game rules. It is penalized by loss of points.

FOUL STROKE: A rules infraction in which the foul takes place as a result of a player's stroke. Example: double contact of the cue tip with the cue ball.

FROZEN: Used to describe balls that are touching each other. When object balls are frozen, they remain in play. When the cue ball is frozen to an object ball, the player proceeds according to the rules of the game being played. A ball resting against a cushion is also said to be frozen.

FULL BALL: The contact of the cue ball with an object ball at its exact center—as opposed to a ball "cut" one-half, one-third, and so on.

HEAD OF TABLE: The short rail marked by the manufacturer's nameplate.

HEAD SPOT: A spot at the midpoint of a line drawn from the side-rail second diamonds of the side rails near the head of the table.

HEAD STRING: A line through the head spot. Most games of pocket billiards start with a break shot from behind this line.

HIGH RUN: The highest consecutive series of scored balls in one inning of a game or tournament.

HOLD: Similar to stop or draw action applied to the cue ball. Any action applied to hold the cue ball back from the course it would normally take.

HUG THE RAIL: When action on the cue ball forces it to roll along or bounce several times against the rail.

INNING: A turn at the table, terminated when a player misses, fouls, scores the maximum number of balls allowed, or ends the game.

KISS: A carom. The cue ball may kiss from one object ball to another. A struck object ball may kiss one or more other object balls.

LAGGING: To determine rotation of play, each player shoots a cue ball from behind the head string to the foot rail and back to the head rail. The player whose ball rests closest to the head rail has the option of shooting first.

LIVE BALL: A ball that is in play under the rules. Also, the cue ball, when its action is "alive" rather than "dead." (*See* DEAD BALL.)

LONG STRING: An imaginary line (drawn for tournament play) from the foot spot to the center of the foot rail, on which balls are spotted when the foot spot is occupied.

MASSÉ: Extreme application of English on the cue ball, accomplished by elevating the cue to nearly perpendicular.

MISCUE: Faulty contact of the cue tip with the cue ball, caused by the tip slipping off its intended point of contact. It is also caused by a defective tip, improper chalking, or a player's unsuccessful attempt to apply excessive English.

MISS: Failure of a player to accomplish his intention on a stroke. Ends an inning and may or may not be a foul, depending on the rules of the game.

NATURAL: A simple shot.

PACK: A cluster of balls at the foot spot either before or after a break shot.

PUSH SHOT: Shoving the cue ball with the tip of the cue, or two contacts of the cue tip on the cue ball. Push shots are legal if the stroke is made with what appears to be one continuous motion. The referee is the sole judge of push-shot legality.

PYRAMID: The placement of object balls in a triangle at the foot spot to start a game.

RACK: A wooden triangle used to arrange object balls in pyramid form at the foot spot to start a game. It also describes the arrangement of object balls after the triangle is removed.

REVERSE: English applied to put "hold" on the ball. It also describes English left, the opposite of "natural," or English right.

ROTATION: The name of a game in which the player must shoot at object balls in numerical order.

RUN: A series of consecutive scores in one inning.

SAFETY: A defensive maneuver that is accomplished when a player sacrifices his opportunity to score, plays "safe" under the rules, ends his turn, and attempts to leave a difficult shot for his opponent.

SCRATCH: Unanticipated development in a stroke that may or may not be a foul, depending on game rules. Pocketing the cue ball is a scratch. Failure to meet specifications of a safety shot also is a scratch.

SETUP: An easy shot.

SNOOKERED: To be unable to shoot the cue ball directly at an object ball.

SPOT BALL: A ball that is placed at the foot, center, or head spot to conform with a rule of play.

SPOT SHOT: When a player shoots at a ball that has been placed on a spot.

SPOTTING: The replacement of balls on the table as required by the rules of the game.

VEE BRIDGE: Used when the bridge must be elevated to shoot over intervening balls.

Know the Rules

HERE is a simplified version of rules for various pocket-billiards games, including 14.1 Continuous Play, the accepted form of league and championship tournament competition. Complete rules are published by the Billiard Congress of America, the official sanctioning and rules-making organization in the game.

14.1 CONTINUOUS PLAY

RACK: The balls are racked on the foot spot with the higher-numbered balls placed in the foot-spot apex of the triangle. Numerical order is not required. A pencil line is drawn around the triangle.

OPENING BREAK: Players lag for break. The player winning the lag has the option of breaking or of forcing his opponent to do so. The starting player must drive two object balls and the cue ball to a cushion, or pocket a called object ball. The penalty for failure to meet these requirements is two points, and the opposing player has the option of accepting the shot or of forcing another break. If two object balls are driven to a cushion and the cue ball is pocketed (scratched), the penalty is one point, and the incoming player has the cue ball "in hand" to shoot from behind the head string.

SCORING: To score, a player must pocket the object ball after indicating that ball by number and the pocket in which it will fall. Any additional balls pocketed on the same stroke are also scored. A player continues at the table until he misses, fouls, plays a safety, or scratches. The first player to reach 150 wins the game or block, if several blocks of 150 form a match. (There are exceptions today to the 150-point game total, particularly in league play. For example, some league rules may limit the number of balls a player may run, perhaps 14, and the number of innings, perhaps 20, for a game total of 280.)

Opening Rack for 14.1

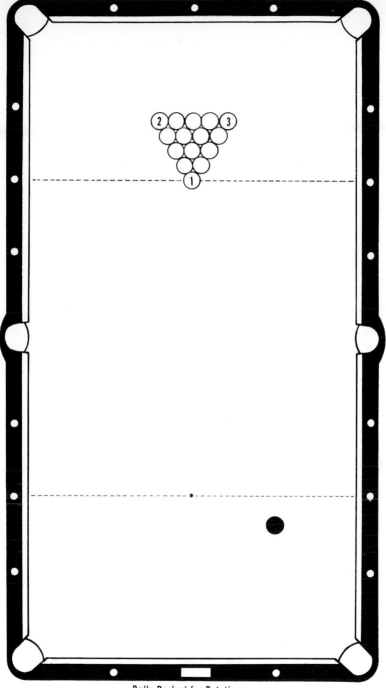

Balls Racked for Rotation

SAFETY PLAY: A player is not obligated to announce his intention to play a safety. Playing a safety requires a player to drive an object ball to a cushion or to drive the cue ball to a cushion after contact with an object ball. Failure to meet the requirements of a safety is termed a scratch, and the penalty is one point.

SCRATCH: A player is charged with a scratch, and the loss of one point, when he fails to meet the requirements of a safety or when the cue ball is pocketed. The penalty for each scratch is one point, but an additional penalty of 15 points is assessed when a player strokes three successive scratches.

PENALTIES: The following is a summary of situations requiring a penalty—the loss of a point or points:

1. Failure to meet opening-break requirements, two points.
2. Shoving the cue ball or touching it with anything but the cue tip, such as the side of the cue or clothing, one point.
3. Playing a scratch, one point.
4. Not having at least one foot touching the floor during a stroke, one point.
5. Stroking while the cue ball or object ball is in motion, one point.
6. Playing three successive scratches, 15 points.

JUMPED BALLS: When the cue ball jumps off the table, the player loses the inning, is penalized one point, and the stroke is termed a scratch. If a called object ball jumps the table, it is respotted, and the player loses the inning without penalty. When a single stroke results in pocketing a called ball and sending another object ball off the table, the jumped ball is respotted and the player continues.

ROTATION

RACK: The balls are racked with the 1-ball on the foot spot, the 2-ball at the left corner, and the 3-ball at the right corner of the full rack.

OPENING BREAK: The players lag for break. The 1-ball is the first object ball. It must be pocketed, or another ball pocketed after cue-ball contact with the 1-ball, or the break-shot player loses the inning.

SCORING: The lowest-numbered ball on the table is the object ball. It must be struck first; otherwise it or any other ball pocketed on the same stroke cannot be scored. All illegally pocketed balls are respotted. The number of a ball is its score value. The game ends when one player or a side reaches 61 points.

EIGHT BALL

RACK: The balls are racked at the foot spot, with the 8-ball at the center of the rack.

OPENING BREAK: The players lag for break. The beginning player need not call a ball on the break. If he does not score, he loses the inning. If he pockets a ball, its number determines his set of future object balls, 1 through 7 or 9 through 15.

SCORING: A player remains at the table until he misses pocketing a ball in his set. The player shooting at the 1-through-7 set must pocket the 1-ball in the right side pocket, as viewed from the head rail. The player shooting at the 9-through-15 set must pocket the 15-ball in the left side pocket. If these balls are not scored in the pockets specified, they must be respotted. After a player pockets all the balls in his set, he must score the 8-ball in a called pocket to win. He loses the game if he pockets the 8-ball before pocketing his set or if he fails to drive the cue ball or the 8-ball to a cushion when shooting to score it.

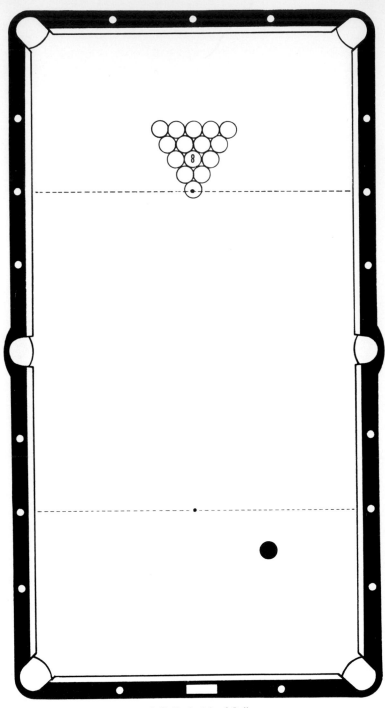

Balls Racked for 8-Ball